LOS ALAMOS REVISITED:
A Workers' History

D1596629

LOS ALAMOS REVISITED:
A Workers' History

by

Peter Malmgren

and Kay Matthews

Wink Books

If you have comments or questions about the book, or wish to purchase, please contact:

Peter Malmgren
PO Box 438, Chimayo NM 87522
petermalmgrennm@gmail.com

FIRST EDITION 2017

Library of Congress Catalog-in-Publication-Data

Los Alamos Revisited: A Workers' History / Peter Malmgren – 1st ed.
Malmgren, Peter (July 12, 1945)
Matthews, Kay (January 22, 1950)
Photos by Peter Malmgren
Historical photos from Los Alamos Laboratory Archives
Cover and book design by Kelly Pasholk, Wink Visual Arts
Published by Wink Books, PO Box 153, El Prado NM 87529
winkbooks.com

Library of Congress Control Number: 2017955927
ISBN: 978-0-9973950-2-0

To the woman who planted the seed in me, who inspired me in life. She spent most of her 100 years fighting for justice, peace, and a more compassionate world. To the memory of my mother, Abigail Malmgreen.

LOS ALAMOS REVISITED

Los Alamos Revisited provides a rare insight into the lives and sacrifices of the ordinary people who made possible the defense work between 1947-2000 to move forward. Author Peter Malmgren, a long-time resident of northern New Mexico and friend to this passing generation, conducted interviews with workers whose personal reflections speak for themselves with clear voices and vivid memories in this oral history reminiscent of Studs Terkel's classic Working.

—**David S. Henkel, Ph.D.**, Emeritus Professor of Planning at the University of New Mexico

I can't applaud enough Peter's efforts to capture and bring to light the stories made by so many people in Northern New Mexico whose sacrifices were hidden for so long. The telling of these stories made all of us aware of the need to always question, and most of all to listen, to truly understand what may lie hidden under veils of secrecy and national security.

—**Johnnye Lewis, Ph.D.**, Director, Center for Native Environmental Health Equity Research

Many of the workers in this book sacrificed their health in creating the Los Alamos Laboratory. Peter Malmgren has tapped into a safe full of secrets within secrets. He unveils a great sense of patriotism and pride in the work that was accomplished. He touches on the sensitive issues of discrimination, and the underlying concerns for health and worker safety.

—**Dimas Chavez**

Dimas started life in Los Alamos in 1943 at the tender age of six. He began his career at the Labs and extended his reach to the State Department and assignments that took him around the world.

CONTENTS

LOS ALAMOS REVISITED

INTRODUCTION

"Los Alamos Revisited," an oral history project, was initiated by the El Rio Arriba Environmental Health Association at Northern New Mexico College in the Española Valley in the year 2000. The project was funded by the University of New Mexico, Center for Population Health, and later by the Center for Disease Control. Its purpose was to tell the story of the creation of Los Alamos from the point of view of the people who helped build it. The historical record is filled with accounts from scientists and pundits, but the voices of the technicians, engineers, trades people, and many others have remained silent. The project recognized this as a significant gap in 20th century New Mexico history and thought it was worth trying to fill.

Little did I know when I raised my hand to volunteer for this oral history project that it would lead to five years of intensive investigation and inquiry. The process of finding these retired workers was a slow and sometimes difficult one. I sought people out one by one and interviewed them in their homes in towns and villages all over northern New Mexico. Having lived in Chimayó for thirty-five years, I started close to home and worked outward, building trust and a network of contacts by word of mouth. The search took me to 25 different communities and involved the testimony of janitors, machinists, radiological technicians, engineers, heavy equipment operators, and senior weapons scientists. Certain themes surfaced in the first year and became recurrent ones in the mounting numbers of transcripts: patriotism, pride in work, discrimination, and concern for health and safety.

Despite the vicissitudes of funding, the project thrived. As of this writing, 150 interviews have been collected, transcribed, and placed in the New Mexico State Records Center and Archives. The photographic exhibit, "Los Alamos Revisited," a collection of 40 archival images of Los Alamos from the formative years, accompanied by text from the oral history study, traveled to a variety of communities. We use the exhibit as a learning tool and a way to heighten public awareness of the workers we chose to honor with this work.

The first workers at Los Alamos had a real sense of mission. Many were World War II veterans. Whatever their job, they felt that they had made a contribution to the war effort and the defeat of Nazi Germany and Japan. Some came back as war heroes and saw Los Alamos as an extension of their military service to the country.

Great efforts were made to recruit people for the early post-war years. The Pro Force (security force), for instance, drew young men from all over the country. They came from the streets of Brooklyn, from the piney woods of Florida, and the farms and homesteads of the Midwest. Mostly they boarded slow-moving trains and headed to Lamy, 18 miles southeast of Santa Fe, with little knowledge of their destination. They were participants in a great mystery, a mission too important to be talked about openly.

They came with a great sense of anticipation. The physical beauty of their new surroundings was over powering. One French woman breathed in that air and likened it to the finest champagne. Evelyn Rose said when the mud got deep she just looked skyward and saw her Shangri-La.

People lived primitively, with wooden boardwalks to help navigate the sea of mud and smoky ovens that burned coal and wood. They worked hard, played hard, and adopted each other as surrogate family. Stephanie Sydoriak described her neighborhood in the western area of town as one where all the houses were wide open and kids circulated from one house to the next with complete freedom. People pitched in to create community. One building served as a church in the morning, a temple in the afternoon, and a dance hall at night. The security fence that surrounded the town was still up and the work was all consuming, but those who came to share in this remarkable undertaking were forging the microcosm of a community.

The buses were being run by the government. They would come to Truchas and many other villages to bring people to work and then return them at night. The Army was still in charge of security in 1947.

Bob Campbell expressed an interesting distinction between the founding fathers of Los Alamos and those, like himself, who came a bit later. Despite his 52 years in the town and his distinguished career as test director both at the Nevada Test Site and the Islands of the Pacific, he says he will always be an outsider. He came after July 16, 1945. It was those select few who built the bomb and tested it in Alamogordo who remain the pioneers and are considered in a special category all their own.

The focus on this recruitment of workers from around the country, however, tended to overlook the Hispanic workers right next door. Of the first five hundred Pro Force employees hired, only four were Hispanic.

Jobs were extremely scarce in 1945 and most men of the Española Valley had traditionally been forced to leave their homes in a seasonal pattern in order to survive. These migrant laborers went to the mines, the railroads, and the sheepherders' camps, leaving the women and children responsible for the farms at home for six months of the year.

Los Alamos changed all that. They no longer had to disrupt their lives by leaving home to seek out hazardous jobs far away and subject their families to the strains of separation and increased labor. This was a profound change in the social patterns of many families, and in most families' opinions, a change for the better. When I asked Josefita Velarde, aged 92, if people were at all hesitant to work in Los Alamos, that secret place where it might be dangerous, she said, "Heck no …we knew all about danger…. Our men risked their lives every day in the mines…. No, they were just glad to have a job where they could go home every night."

Many also viewed work at Los Alamos as an opportunity to demonstrate their ability to take on technical challenges and excel, instilling a sense of pride. But they were slower to gain recognition for their work and proper remuneration as compared to their Anglo counterparts. This sometimes had to do with a discrepancy in educational achievement. "I can do the work, but without the diploma I get no recognition." Yet they were given the opportunity to work at a level that would have been undreamed of in the outside world. The machinists were not only extraordinary technicians, but many also did design work. A scientist would scribble a drawing on a napkin, plunk it down on the workbench, and ask if it could be made. They often had to design and build new tools to meet these challenges. The technicians and scientists worked more closely together in those early years, as Gene Westerhold put it, "shoulder to shoulder," and there was mutual respect and camaraderie. As the Lab grew larger and more stratified, those early bonds unfortunately were broken.

The theme of pride in one's work is a strong thread that ties the stories together from people of all levels of expertise and a variety of disciplines. We hear legendary tales of scientists who brought cots into the Lab and often didn't bother to go home, working through the night. Or others who woke up at 3:00 a.m. with a notion about how to solve a problem and hightailed it over to the Lab, unwilling to wait for morning. Other examples of dedication and pride come from those who commuted long distances every day, in all kinds of weather. Joe Mascareñas began work every single day at 7:30 in the morning, traveling forty miles from Dixon and never expecting any extra compensation. Harold Archuleta, one of the most respected plutonium specialists from TA-55, the plutonium facility, would routinely work until 9:00 at night when procedures required it. Others showed their energy and enthusiasm for overtime and hazard pay. Work in the restricted areas meant another 35 cents an hour. Jonathan Garcia had a young family and worked all the overtime he could muster.

Another pattern that emerges is disturbing. As long as you were healthy and productive and an asset to the Lab, you tended to thrive, but once an illness struck you were quickly considered expendable. For those foolhardy enough to demand compensation for their health care, the results were predictably dire. They say you can't fight the government and by that they mean the Lab. Jay Hammel put up a short and dignified struggle as he was dying of thyroid cancer. Despite a long and distinguished career in low temperature physics, he failed to convince the powers that be that his early exposures in the Pacific were the cause of his fatal illness.

For those who worked a long career and managed to dodge the bullet of ill health, the benefits were substantial. One woman sat vigil with her dying husband who had contracted a particularly gruesome skin disease that made his flesh separate and fall off the bone. His last words to her included thoughts about the Laboratory: "You may feel a need to try and blame the Lab for my illness and claim compensation. But don't do it. The Lab was good to me and my family for 40 years and regardless of what happened, we are owed nothing."

Another man, considerably younger and still in relatively good health, had worked as a radiological technician all his life. At age 54 he reflects on his working life and his future with an air of resignation: "I've been in every building in the Laboratory and been exposed to all sorts of things. It's been a good job and provided well for my family, but I know it is going to kill me. I can accept that knowledge. I knew the risks going in and I made my choices. Now it's just a matter of time."

Not everyone shares this man's sense of resignation. There are countless workers, living and dead, who recognized that salaries and benefits can't be measured against debilitating illness. A list of those who were believed to have died of work related illnesses, remembered by interviewees, is displayed in the photo exhibit and at the end of this book.

There are growing numbers of workers who have contracted serious illnesses and need help with their escalating medical expenses. Jonathan Garcia contracted leukemia while he was still in his early 40s. A bone marrow transplant saved his life, but his health problems continue. He was a heavy equipment operator at Area G, the hot dump, where every conceivable type of toxic waste is buried. Jonathan, along with hundreds of others, struggled against governmental bureaucracy to get what is their due from the Energy Employees Occupational Illness Compensation Program Act (EEOICPA): $150,000 in cash and lifetime medical benefits. Unfortunately, the Act requires that workers with diminished strength and mounting anger and frustration prove their cases by providing medical and work histories that are often difficult to obtain. The burden of proof remains on the shoulders of these men as the program grinds on and men start to die waiting for relief.

A group called the Los Alamos POWs, Project for Workers' Safety, was formed in 2000 to help fight for the rights of the workers who were seeking compensation for work related health problems. The group, under the leadership of Ben Ortiz and Jerry Leyba, met on the last Wednesday of every month at the Johnson Control Small Business Center on Railroad Avenue, directly across from the Community College in Española.

One hundred and fifty workers provide us with a mosaic of opinion, not a consensus on the meaning of Los Alamos. The blacks and whites have long since dissolved into infinite gradations of grey. One man simply stated that as for the Lab, "We can't live with it and we can't live without it."

Working on this project certainly made my perception of Los Alamos more multi-dimensional as well. When I go to a protest with the anti-nuke people, as I have been doing throughout my life, my perception has shifted. Many people want to shut down Area G, or the whole Lab for that matter, concerned about the environmental threat that we all acknowledge. For me it's a little more complicated. What's very important, even beyond the ecological issues, is the human cost, meaning the loss of jobs. Villages like my own would dry up and blow away if this economic engine stopped chugging. We've all become addicted to the Lab. If you were to stand out on State Highway 76 in the early morning and count the cars that were heading to Los Alamos, you would count in the thousands.

The last time I went to a protest in Los Alamos the most powerful part of the day for me was sitting in a small side room near the pond and hearing the words of two elderly Japanese survivors of Hiroshima. With the help of a translator, the man and woman said they have dedicated the remaining years of their lives to getting people not to forget them. They've become an embarrassment to the Japanese government. They have had to struggle to receive any compensation for all their years of suffering. The woman had never been to America before, but here she was in the Lion's Den, having come to the place that ruined her life, with the courage to be able to speak with us and to try to reach out in a very gracious way.

AN OVERVIEW OF THE BOOK:

ORIGINS

Tracing workers' roots seemed a likely place to start my inquiry. Many came from far and wide, across this vast country, and others came from the Valley nearby. These were two parallel streams of labor, a wide range of experience and education, all merging into the melting pot that was the Manhattan Project.

WORK

This is the heart of the book. What did you do every day and how did you feel about it? Many told me there were times that they spent more of their waking hours at work than at home with their families. This was an intense commitment. I have a close neighbor, Robert Martinez, who misses his years on the job and turns his exercising machine on the porch toward the Lab so that he can remember all the good times. Many loved their work, like Robert, and others grinned and bore it for the sake of the family.

BOMB TESTING

Bomb testing was a specific chapter in Lab history that occurred in the South Sea Islands and then at the Nevada Test

Site. Thousands were involved. Untold numbers were exposed to high levels of contamination in the testing process. It was the beginning of the Cold War and patriotism ran high. This was considered critically important work for the security of the nation.

HEALTH AND SAFETY

Health and safety was a topic that popped up repeatedly in the interviews. Men would often reflect on the fact that they were the lone survivor of a crew of six or more. Their fellow crewmembers died young and often of cancer. The list of men who died in the line of duty grew longer and longer as the interviews continued. And it wasn't just janitors and techs who were on that list—it also included a number of young scientists. They took dangerous risks in their drive to get the work done very quickly. Many of them paid the ultimate price.

WHISTLEBLOWERS

This a chapter devoted to three men who stood up to the all-powerful Lab and said no. They were fighting for workers' rights and against the RIF (Reduction in Force of 1995) that discriminated against Hispanic workers. They managed to retain their jobs but were forever branded as agitators and wore a "target" on their backs for years to come.

GENE WESTERHOLD

I devote a chapter to the man who I considered one of the most extraordinary individuals of the group of 150. His personal character, courage, and loyalty are immediately apparent. He took on difficult tasks and risked his life in a criticality accident that took the life of Cecil Kelly. Yet Gene never complained, followed orders, and always remained positive. He was repaid at the end of 44 years of service by being denied access to his extensive medical records. They must have thought him a troublemaker for having asked for them.

CONCLUSION

In the final chapter I pay tribute to those who have died in the 15 years that have passed since the interviews were conducted.

Peter Malmgren,
Chimayó, New Mexico 2017

Chapter One

ORIGINS

Los Alamos Laboratory was conceived by J. Robert Oppenheimer and Brigadier General Leslie Groves as they walked through the forests of the Los Alamos Ranch School on the northern New Mexico Pajarito Plateau in the summer of 1942. General Groves, commander of the Manhattan District of the Corps of Engineers, had hired Oppenheimer, a University of California theoretical physicist, to lead a group of scientists who would design and build a nuclear weapon after the outbreak of World War II. Groves was assigned the task of finding a site for a new laboratory where this weapon could be developed. Major John Dudley, who worked for Groves, had already recommended a site closer to Jemez Springs.

But Oppenheimer, who had a summer home near Pecos, didn't like the Jemez Springs location and took Groves and Dudley, on horseback, to Los Alamos, "cottonwoods" in Spanish. That night Groves made the decision to locate what became known as the Manhattan Project on the remote Ranch School site, surrounded by a former Mexican land grant and Hispanic homesteads. Once the decision was made, the Ranch was quickly shuttered and a substantial number (150 families) of the homesteading farmers were kicked off their land.

This story of dispossession is rarely discussed in the histories of the founding of the city of Los Alamos and the development of

Oppenheimer in Japan in 1960.

Los Alamos National Laboratory. The Pajarito Plateau was first home to Pueblo Indians, whose prehistoric ruins surround the town and Laboratory and whose descendants live in the neighboring pueblos of San Ildefonso and Santa Clara. The Ramón Vigil land grant, dating from 1742, lies just south of site of the Los Alamos Ranch School. Detroit businessman Ashley Pond, whose name is familiar to current day Los Alamos residents as the small pond in the center of town, bought the Vigil grant and ran a dude ranch there until 1917, when the water source dried up. He subsequently bought land north of the grant and built the Los Alamos Ranch School, which operated from 1917 to 1942, as a Boy Scout-like private school.

In December of 1942 the Secretary of War wrote the ranch director a letter stating, "You are advised that it has been determined necessary to the interests of the United States in the prosecution of the War that the property of the Los Alamos Ranch School be acquired for military purposes." The school was compensated by the government at fair market value and received $335,000 plus interest.

The Hispanic farmers and ranchers who homesteaded much of the land surrounding the Ranch School were also ordered to leave and received a fraction of the school's compensation. According to historian Malcolm Ebright, "the total amount of appraised value for all buildings and improvements of the twenty-three homesteaders was about $4,900 ... 1/20th of the land values the government agreed to for the school." (Malcolm Ebright, "Hispanic Homesteaders on the Pajarito Plateau; An Unconstitutional Taking of Property at Los Alamos 1942-1945," *La Jicarita News*, May 2007, pp 4-5, 8.) Ebright also found that "the procedures followed in evicting the homesteaders were often appalling." In some instances the Army Corps of Engineers showed up at the homesteaders' properties with rifles, ordered their immediate eviction, and decimated homes, outbuildings, and corrals. This is Emelina Grant, one of the interviewees, describing what happened to her family on Pajarito Mesa:

"My husband was in World War 1 and he had a chance to get 160 acres to farm. We had a crop and everything ready. My husband had a team of horses and cows and we had to turn them loose. We didn't have a place for them down here where we are living now. They brought the soldiers there. We had to move. I don't know why. They didn't explain anything. When we left we left in a hurry. They gave us so many days to move. We gathered what we could in the truck. I had a big box, a shoebox filled with pictures. When we went back a few days later to get more stuff, I found my pictures all scattered and torn. Nobody else but the soldiers had been there. They got into everything and that made me mad. Like I said we let the horses and cows roam free, but the pig was unlucky, he didn't live very long. I didn't know that sour milk can kill a pig. I gave him the sour milk and pretty soon I heard the squeals. It was the pig dying with the bellyache. I didn't even know."

In today's dollars the estimated value of the homesteaders' land is $6,679,633. In the mid-1990s a handful of surviving homesteaders and the heirs of many others organized the Pajarito Plateau Homesteaders Association, which filed two lawsuits, one that addressed the loss of land and the other alleging human rights violations. The latter suit claimed that some of the homesteaders were forced to labor on construction of the Manhattan Project without proper compensation and were subjected to medical experimentation by being exposed to high levels of radiation. The government dismissed both lawsuits on the basis that the statute of limitations had expired. Eventually the homesteaders were able to pursue their compensation claim before Congress, and in 2004 were offered a $10 million settlement. The Association accepted the settlement, although several heirs believe that a more equitable settlement would amount to $60 million.

According to Joe Gutierrez, one of the founders of the Homesteaders Association and who is interviewed in the Whistleblowers section, "Part of the injustice was that this particular issue has never been documented, written about. It's always been kept secret. I want to raise the consciousness of people that you have to stand up for your rights. Apart from that, there was a clear injustice done that needs to be acknowledged and corrected. The other goal is the genuine attempt to get some form of reparation. If we don't prevail on the land issue we hope for some form of compensation that begins to correct the disparity that was experienced."

After acquisition of the school property and homesteaders' lands, the need for labor, both skilled and unskilled, to build the Laboratory was immediate, and two streams of that labor eventually developed. A large pool of labor came from the Hispanic farmers of the Espanola Valley; the second source of workers was drawn from all over the country and beyond our very shores.

Scientists were recruited from the east and the capitals of Europe. Security guards came from the south with barely the shoes on their feet. Technicians came from the midlands and soldiers from far and wide. Gilbert Fuentes, from the mountain village of Truchas, struggled to become one of the first Hispanics to join the ranks of the 500 security guards who were hired. Men like Gilbert, who returned from WWII as decorated war heroes, were expecting some consideration in hiring. They were sorely disappointed. As the numbers of those hired grew exponentially in the first years, the door opened very slowly to the local Hispanic workers compared to the others.

In this chapter I want to look into the origins from these two streams of labor as they poured into Los Alamos: "With a clutter of barracks, trailers, and huts, Los Alamos was bursting at the seams. In January 1943 the population was 1,500. By the end of 1944, it had quadrupled to 5,675, and by 1945 it would be 8,200." (Eileen Welsome, *The Plutonium Files: America's Secret Medical Experiments in the Cold War*, The Dial Press, 1999, p. 73) Many of those who came were without a clue as to their final destination. They put down the plow and climbed the Hill for the rest of their working lives.

MANUEL SALAZAR—*Disposal Supervisor*

Manuel Salazar

My family moved to Gunnison, Colorado from our farm in Velarde, New Mexico, where we had 1,000 apple trees and large chile fields. My father's job was to place the railroad in a location for mining some secret metal that was vital for the war effort. He built the RR from Gunnison to Baldwin and was in charge of 150 men. My mother was the cook for the extra gang. We lived in railroad cars. The men slept six or eight to a car, my mother cooked for 50 to 60 a day. She had big boilers, broilers, and kerosene stoves that were set up in one of the cars. Three or four cars had long tables where the men ate. They were Yugoslavian, Austrian, Colored, Spanish, Mexican, and Anglo.

After we came back to New Mexico I was a student on a summer work program and my job was to clean out a fleet of school buses at Los Alamos. They were parked near the PX, so as I scrubbed and swept I could watch the young scientists come and go to lunch. One day a man in a funny hat rode up on a bicycle but it was unlike anything I had ever seen. It was long and skinny and looked as fast as the wind. One day I screwed up my courage and approached the man as he came for lunch and asked him if I might take this marvelous machine for a ride. The man replied, "As long as you get it back when lunch is over you may ride it." So off I went and for a magical 30 minutes I flew around the Lab. It was only years later that someone pointed out to me who that man in the funny hat was—Robert Oppenheimer.

RAY CASIAS—*Water Specialist*

I was raised among the Indians of San Juan Pueblo. My grandfather established himself there as a blacksmith, fixing plows and wagon wheels for over 70 years. I displayed musical talent at an early age and one time when I was five the nuns dressed me up in a tiny mariachi suit and plunked me down on the stage to perform. I sang all my life. I had a live radio show in Santa Fe, and later on I turned to gospel.

In those days, I guess my daddy sort of carried a tradition with him. They have a boy and they say, you are going to become a man at a young age. So you can be a man all your life, not afraid of work, etc. Say there was a sheepherder and he owned a lot of sheep. So my dad said, "Well I have a boy here, he's ten years old. Do you want to take him with you? Take him up to the mountains." "Well, how much are we going to pay the boy?" "Twenty dollars a month." So here, without asking me to agree to go, they sent me up to Tierra Amarilla and to the mountains about thirty miles up. I didn't know where in the world I was. I was taking care of sheep at the age of ten for twenty dollars a month.

My oldest brother was there too, with a cowboy. He gave me a bunch of firecrackers. "When ever you spot a coyote, just light one of these." That's the way I used to scare the coyotes away.

The *caporal* did the cooking. In the evening we would bring the sheep in. There was no corral. They moved the camp con-

Ceta Tafoya, 61 years old, former governor of Santa Clara Pueblo, serving soup at the East Cafeteria at LANL.

stantly. He would take care of the meals in the morning and the evening. Maybe pack you a little lunch and send you out.

I was in a deep old canyon and it was kind of sad being there all by myself. I started crying. I wanted to go home. Caporal was kind of strict. At that time I was talking to him and I told him I wanted to go home. Here was a coyote about two hundred feet away, up on a little ridge. He said, see that coyote over there? Watch him. He pulled his gun out and bam, he killed him dead. If you don't keep quiet, if you don't shut your mouth about that crying business, that's what's going to happen to you!

So I stayed another week and when the big boss came, they told him that I didn't want to stay no more. That's when they took me back and dropped me at the bus depot, bought my ticket. I hadn't taken a bath in a month. I had a wool jacket that was torn all over. I wish I had a picture of me. They sent me to the bus and it was really dark out there where the turn off to Chamita and El Duende is. It was 10:00 at night and I had to walk home in the dark. I was scared. This happened in the springtime.

I remember looking in the window into one of the rooms where my mother was. The house was almost buried underground. I kept looking through that window, I was afraid to go in. I wasn't afraid of my mom, but I afraid of my dad. I knew he wouldn't be at all happy. He was pretty strict.

The story about my great grandma was that she was kidnapped out of Navajo country and brought to San Juan and sold for a horse. The Trujillos adopted her. She was said to have been 16 at the time of her capture and expecting a child. That made my grandma a full blood, my mom a half blood, and me one quarter.

RUBEN MONTOYA—*Metallurgist, Sigma Building*

I was born in 1923 in Santa Fe and raised by my grandparents and three uncles. One was a master bookbinder. He had me working for 15 cents an hour. To start off, they would print the pages on big sheets. The corners were numbered and then there was a method of folding them that brought the pages into sequence. Then they would put these folded sheets in a vise and cut them. Then my mother would sew them together in a special fashion. Later the pages were trimmed, then put in the vise again and hit with a big hammer. He hit the side to give the curvature of the binding. Then they were glued with gauze to reinforce the glue and a leather binding to finish the job.

The Lab approached my uncle to work for them. They sent guards down to Santa Fe with all the necessary materials to his place on Cerrillos Road and he would do the binding there. Every night they would take all the scraps and all the work that he had done back to Los Alamos. In the morning they would bring it all back. He continued that way until he finished the job. They wanted him to set up a shop on the Hill, but he said, "No way, if you want me to do the work for you, it will be done here, in Santa Fe."

ESTEFANITA MARTINEZ—*Storyteller, Home Care*

Estefanita Martinez

I think I had the best childhood in the village because all the adults were watching over us. We belonged to every grownup who lived in the pueblo [San Juan]. It made it nice, no matter where you were, if you hurt yourself and were crying there was always someone to comfort you, dry up your tears, and set you on your way again. So I treasure my life with my grandmother and grandfather. One thing that they always taught me was to talk to people, even if you didn't know them. It is important that we speak to people.

We stayed home a lot; we didn't have a car. We had a wagon and a team of horses. My grandfather used to plow the land with those horses and bring in the harvest. He would stop at the homes of the needy and drop off corn to be husked. Indian corn comes in all different colors. If you planted white corn for posole one always ended up spotted because someone had blue corn in a nearby field and the pollen came over and you got spotted ones, red and yellow. It was nice to husk the Indian corn. You'd get your tamale husks while you were doing it. The thin ones closest to the corn were cut into squares and saved to roll the *punche* [grandpa's tobacco] in.

My grandmother even gathered the pollen. Grandfather would tell her that he was almost out of pollen and she would fetch her pottery plate, especially made for gathering pollen. She would get the tassel and tap it. Bugs and everything would fall on the plate. She would use a piece of the tassel to sweep away the bugs and leave only the pollen in place. When she had enough it would go into a small bottle and given to grandpa, that he used in ceremonies.

DICK MONEY—*Chemist*

I was born in Chicago on the South Side, 61st and Spalding in 1921. My father was a civil engineer who built grain elevators until the 1929 crash. I got interested in music in high school. It was Prohibition times and "taverns" sprung up all over Chicago. A stein of beer was a nickel, a pack of cigarettes 11 cents. Jukeboxes hadn't come in yet, so if you were out for a drink and some dancing you relied on live music. Although only a freshman in high school, I landed a job in one of these joints.

I'm a drummer and I was making two bucks a night, big money in 1935. I was small of stature and couldn't compete athletically with the big Polish and Irish kids, so I relied on my music. I was offered a job in a ballroom band, a real step up, but my father put his foot down. He was determined I would follow in his footsteps and attend Purdue University. I ended up studying chemistry and followed that profession to Los Alamos, but I never lost my love of the music and at the age of 80 I'm still performing.

FELIX DE PAULA—*Trinity*

I enjoyed everything about growing up in Brooklyn, New York. At nine I borrowed my brother's shoeshine box and went out for a nickel a shine. Then we progressed to little wagons full of vegetables and went door to door. Later I was working in a quilting factory manufacturing Army jackets for the boys overseas (later all five of us boys were to serve). We had the theater real close by, and there was Manhattan where you could go to the Paramount Theater and see the well-known stars, the singers, the big bands, all for 25 cents!

During the depression the Civilian Conservation Corps came in and things were looking a little better. At least some people were working instead of just walking the streets. My father had a very hard time of it. Because of the lack of money, he did what so many others were doing, which was doing as much as possible at home to save on expenses. He would put soles and heels on our shoes. We would get a new pair when school started and they had to last us through the following year. He was repairing shoes one day and put a pot of glue on the stove that had hardened and that he wanted to melt. He went in to listen to his favorite "Amos and Andy" radio show and remembered that he had not taken the lid off of the glue pot. He ran to the stove to turn it off and as he reached across the stove the darn thing exploded and covered his fingers with molten glue. It fused the fingers together and crippled the hand.

He lived that way for four years until he found a surgeon, a Jewish man. The doctor told my father after examining him, "You know you don't have any bone damage. It is all fused skin. I could go ahead and operate but it's expensive." Well, we didn't have the money. We had to raise $1,000 for the surgery and $500 for the hospital. Well, we discovered we could get the hospital fee down if my mother acted as his nurse.

My father notified the doctor that we could take care of the hospital costs and were trying to raise the $1,000 but it was nearly impossible. That represented a man's wages for an entire year. Anyway, sometime later the surgeon drove up to the house and said to my father, "I can't go through life knowing that I could have made you a working citizen again, able to support your family. So I will operate for free." He went ahead and the operation was a great success.

RICHARD CHAPMAN—*Fire Chief*

Dad transferred from Tennessee out to New Mexico in the 1930s to work on the Conchas Dam. He was the maintenance foreman for the vehicle shop and stayed for three years. At the dam site they had a nice living area. There were three or four family dwellings for all the federal employees. But most of the workers—the laborers, the carpenters, and the contract workers—lived out in a place called "Rag City." They lived in tents and shanties—it was 1937. It wasn't much of a living out at Rag City—that's about what it was, a rag city—but at least they had work.

In later years dad took over the management of the fishing lodge at El Vado Lake. We'd cut ice on the river and store it in bunkers with earthen mounds over them. We'd start cutting ice into blocks when it was about two feet thick and stick them in the bunkers, leaving an inch gap between them. When there was lots of snow we'd chink the ice with the snow so the blocks wouldn't stick together. Then we covered them with two inches of snow, then a layer of sawdust, and then a final layer of snow.

My dad was quite a mechanic. He rigged up a circular saw with a lever that lowered and raised the blade. It sure beat the old two-man saw. In the summer we'd take out the ice blocks, hose them down, and sell them for drinks or to preserve the fish catch. We sold it by the pound. It didn't amount to much money, but money went a long ways then.

REYNAL MAESTAS—*Construction*

I was born in Rio Oso, New Mexico, up in the mountains in the back of a horse wagon. My mother was lying there with my sisters Anna and Porfiria, but I couldn't wait to get home. I wanted to see the world. I started school in Chilili when I was ten and took a job as the classroom monitor for $12 a month. I had to get there early and get that potbelly going so the place would be warm by the time the teacher arrived. In the winter when the snows were heavy, Dad would get up really early, cut down a tree, and drag it along the trail to school. That's how he plowed a path for us!

When it was too cold, I would go and build up the fire in the morning, then I would go later to keep the fire going. We used to carry lunch from home. There was another Maestas family that brought their lunch. Well heck, during this time people were very poor. They brought some beans in a five pound bucket, but they forgot to poke holes in the lid. They were kind of ashamed for us to see it, but we all warmed what we brought on the top of the stove. The stove was a good one, and it really put out the heat. Before we knew it the beans exploded and we had beans on the ceiling. It was quite a mess. We cleaned it up as best we could and when the teacher returned from lunch, she asked, "Did somebody burn the beans?"

GENE BARRINGTON—*Machinist*

I came from the piney woods of Florida and a one-room shack with wooden shutters instead of glass—for all nine of us. My father was a Methodist preacher and he had a 100-acre piece of land—sandy, piney woods mainly. We could mainly grow sweet potatoes, peanuts, and sugarcane. There was an old hermit who lived in a ramshackle shack that was worse than ours. He built a raft in the dry woods just like he was going to float down the Mississippi. So, I built one too. I had a lot of fun with that raft. I went with Huckleberry Finn and Tom Sawyer down the river.

It helped that I had a whole set of manual training books that belonged to my uncle when he was in school. He passed them along to me and he didn't realize what I was, a builder.

RAYMOND MAESTAS—*Technician*

Raymond Maestas

I lost my leg as a child. I had a lot of pain in my ankle and it started swelling up. The doctor in Santa Fe figured out what it was and in 20 days I had lost my leg. It was a very rare sarcoma. My little sister, who was three years younger, developed it in her left leg, in the exact same bone. The sarcoma spread to her lungs and her heart and she died at age sixteen. I am going on my 40th year of using an artificial leg, mid-thigh.

I managed to attend high school and get a summer job at Los Alamos. I got sent to UNM-LA for an associate's degree in electrical engineering. I also studied strain gauges.

Take any metal, if it is stretched or hammered on, it will record how many G's it gives out, how much strain the metal can tolerate. The gauges are tiny and the metal that they are attached to has to be polished like a mirror. Placing the gauge is the tricky part. You have to leave the metal surface like glass, then place the epoxy, and then the wiring (thin as a human hair). Then a charge is placed inside the vessel, detonated, and the gauges record the force that was absorbed.

They once sent me to the Nevada test Site to attach some gauges because of the 2,000 men who worked there, no one could manage such a delicate job. I was always very skilled with my hands. I could repair anything that was put in front of me.

VIRGINIA STOVALL—*A Living Treasure of Los Alamos*

I was born in Indianapolis, Indiana in 1909. My grandfather raised horses and on Sunday morning liked to go up to Meridian St. in Indianapolis and watch the people come and go in their horse and buggies. This was in the 1880s. He was over there one morning and Mr. Pearson of the Pearson Piano Company was standing nearby admiring the horses. He said that he wished he could get one like that. Grandfather immediately suggested that they make a deal. He was well known as a horse trader. He told Pearson that he would give him his prized horse if he would in turn hand over his best piano.

Not long after this talk grandfather entered the showroom and was offered anything he saw. He inquired as to where the very best one in the store was. It was in the back room, an ebony Steinway upright. So they made their trade. Grandfather had three daughters, one of whom was my mother, and he wanted them to have the best education that they could get.

I graduated from the Western College for Women in Oxford, Ohio. My husband studied with Edward Teller at George Washington University and was asked to come to Los Alamos in 1947. We came out on the limited train to save money. It took three days and two nights. Then a man sidled up to us at Lamy and whispered for us to follow him. He had a dilapidated Army sedan and took us to 109 E. Palace and then up the mountain to our new home.

DARLEEN ORTIZ—*Daughter of Max Ortiz, Janitor*

I was born in Los Alamos in 1955. My father, Max Ortiz, was hired in 1947 to build roads. From there he went to Zia [Los Alamos contracting company] on the janitorial staff and stayed until his retirement in 1975. He used to hunt and fish a lot. I learned how to do both from him. We used to go to the pond and fish underneath a bridge. There were tons of fish. We also fished all the streams that were nearby. For deer he preferred to go into the restricted areas where the game was larger. He did the same when he gathered piñon—we found them oversized in all the wrong places.

We used to eat so much that grew wild around us. I can't imagine that some of it wasn't contaminated. We used to eat wild strawberries, acorns, piñon nuts, and monkey nuts, tiny nuts with furry bottoms and tiny seeds inside. We also ate flowers, like the ones they put in salads now. We didn't have snacks. As a matter of fact, we were hungry a lot of the time and would eat roses, carnations, and this little red and orange flower that Mom grew that smelled like cloves. Mom would treat ice to make her homemade snow ice cream. We always drank from the ice-cold streams, of course. I did that until I was ready to graduate from high school.

MYRTLE WHITE ROMERO—*Medical Technician*

I was born in 1908 La Hart, Kansas. While I was still small, my poppa, who was a smelter worker, was sent from his job in Iola to the nearby town of Bartlesville, Oklahoma. Grandpa and Grandma went with us.

My mother moved back to Shannuck, Kansas after my father was murdered. It happened on his way home from work from the smelter in 1913 when I was five years old. A detective from the cement company worked on the case for five years and couldn't solve the mystery. One time when we were still living in Bartlesville, Poppa had a couple of drunks arrested for using foul language in front of the women of the family. When they were drunk they were belligerent and when they were sober they were ashamed. Poppa worked the nightshift and walked a long way home to our little house in the country. He was killed at the depot as he was walking out towards the railroad tracks.

One morning he didn't come home. Grandma sent one of the kids to find out what had happened. When he got to the depot there was a huge crowd assembled. He pushed through and saw his father lying dead on the ground. He had been shot in the head and the heart with 36 cents in his pocket. It wasn't any holdup. As I said, the detectives worked for five long years and couldn't give us an answer.

JOSEFITA VELARDE—*Medical Technician*

I was born in 1911 and started school in Chimayó in 1917. Then in January of 1918 we moved to Leadville, Colorado. Our intention was never to settle in Leadville. We went there to clear up our debts like everyone else. My parents were both educated at the Menaul Mission School. But despite his education, my father couldn't support a growing family on a teacher's salary. There was a brief job that was challenging. He did the federal census from Santa Fe up to the Colorado border on horseback. He had to ford the Rio Ojo Caliente holding his large ledgers well over his head to protect them from the rushing waters.

Well, I started in a one-room schoolhouse in Leadville right next to the smelter. My father worked there and we lived only a half block away. It was far from a city or even a town; it was just a bunch of houses strung out along the road. No one in my school spoke English very well. We were Mexican, Croatian, Serbian, Yugoslavian, and American. There were also first-generation Europeans born here.

Our family grew until we were nine. They were born every 15 to 18 months. We lived in a pretty exciting household because my father was always offering help to the newcomers. "Mano Miguel, I'm having a problem. Mano Miguel, do you think you could help me?" People from Chimayó, Taos, and Peñasco all came for work and my father was their lifeline. He helped with housing, jobs, and legal issues.

My mother provided meals to the new arrivals. She baked in a large wood stove, making six loaves at a time. Her monthly flour order was 200 lbs. for $3.00. We had two fulltime boarders to add to her numbers. There was never a dull moment or empty chair at our dinner table.

I spent my childhood and early adult years in this rainbow-like community. I met and married my husband there and finally settled in Española on a lovely four-acre ranch. We both gravitated to the Lab. I found work as a medical technician. I'm sure you've heard of this a number of times, but the Lab has been an absolute lifesaver. If that place ever closed down it would be a catastrophe. There wasn't much here before they came. The men had to go out for work all the time. The only way this area survived up until then is the feeling that the people have for their land, a mystical feeling. This rootedness, like my father feeling that he was always in exile because he couldn't get back home.

When we would make special trips down in the fall to see relatives and share in the harvest, the first thing that struck him as he approached the town was the smell—of roasting chile, the sweet fragrance of fruit, flowers, and vegetables. If only briefly, he was home.

BERNARD RYAN—*Baseball Star*

I was born and raised in Leadville, Colorado on Dec. 23, 1923. My dad was James Ryan from Ireland. My mother was Bridget Allen of Irish extraction but born in Toledo, Ohio. So I feel that I'm full-blooded Irish.

My dad died when I was six years old in 1930, the heart of the depression. He was a miner and suffered from miner's consumption. Pneumonia set in and in those days that was almost an automatic killer. I was the last of eleven children. Things sort of turned around when Roosevelt was elected in 1932. The mines were all shut down; they were full of water and inoperable. I remember when the WPA [Work Project Administration] came in. They had government funds to build a swimming pool. Now Leadville needed a swimming pool like it needed another mine dump, but it did put people to work. Fathers and sons who had jumped freight trains in search of work came back in search of those precious government jobs. People were walking down main street with a little spring in their step and a little jingle in their pocket. Things were starting to change.

FRANK OSVATH—*Machinist*

I was born and raised in Detroit, Michigan. My parents came from Hungary back in 1915. I went to the Henry Ford Trade School during the depression. My mother sent me there not just to learn but to earn!

We started in the 8th grade and went through high school. We primarily concentrated on mechanical subjects. We worked in the machine shop for two weeks and then did academics for one week, and so on. We got paid to do this. The parts that we practiced on were the same ones from the car's assembly line. Years later I went back to see the place and it was all boarded up. They said it had to close because Henry Ford was violating child labor laws. I started at ten cents an hour with two cent raises at every report card. When I was finished with my four-year stint I was up to nearly a dollar!

Chapter Two

WORK

It took an army of machinists, health specialists, painters, janitors, weapons technicians, pyro-chemical technicians, pipe-fitters, radiation cloud samplers, administrators, welders, chemists, engineers, photographers, physicists, plutonium specialists, medical technicians, RCTs [radiological control technicians], Pro Force security, construction workers, computer experts, foundry workers, nurses, hot dump disposal people, nuclear test workers, mathematicians, surveyors, metallurgists, and slews of secretaries. It took all these specific skills to make the bomb, test it, and use it to end the war. General Grove, who co-directed the Manhattan Project with Robert Oppenheimer, was a fanatic when it came to security. He wanted the workers kept in the dark about what they were working on so the secret never leaked out. He did this by compartmentalizing the work into separate procedures. One person would work in his or her own little cubicle doing one stage of a lengthy process without a clue about the end product. On the other hand, the scientists were all in the know from day one. They were trusted to keep the Lab's great secret while the overwhelming number of people labored in ignorance. Felix De Paula was a young soldier who was sent to the Trinity bomb-testing site for months leading up to the test. He struggled with intense heat and brutal living conditions and knew nothing of the mission until that fateful day when the bomb was detonated.

Hispanic workers came to the Lab in the early years with very little formal education and were no match for their Anglo counterparts. Those who managed to excel did so on the strength of their native intelligence. The technicians worked closely with the scientists early on and often solved problems for them but rarely got credit for their critical work, although scientists knew how much they relied on the techs' abilities.

The fact was that it took a large number of dedicated and skilled workers to provide the support system for the scientists who typically received all of the credit. Bob Campbell, director of all testing in the Pacific Islands as well as the Nevada Test Site, has a different perspective. He said that a number of the lead scientists on the test site lost track of the critical function that large numbers of workers provided in support of their goals. They took it for granted. He chastened them for this high-handed attitude and stated flatly that without this network of support nothing would have been accomplished.

This is Ray Maestas, technician:

"I built a lot of instruments that were involved with the bomb rack. The instruments consisted of power supplies and recording devices. Unfortunately, most of them were blown up along with the bomb. The engineer would give me the schematic and the parts list. I would go to the warehouse, order the parts, both metal and electronic, and build the whole thing from scratch. Like building a TV, only this one had to be done in two weeks. Then, let's see if it works, if it does, let's take it to Nevada, hook it up and fire.

"You were judged in Los Alamos by how much you knew and how good your education was. If you were a PhD you weren't going to say 'good morning' to a technician. You would meet one face to face and he wouldn't say a word. But later on, when he needed your help, he'd sing a different tune.

"A scientist isn't going to dirty his hands. He doesn't even know how to operate a lathe. He'd smash his fingers. Between the engineer and me, he designed it and I built it, but he got all the credit for the work. I did all the electrical and mechanical work, all he did was a design. I should have gotten some credit, but I got nothing."

This is Ruben Montoya, metallurgical specialist:

"In one week I was welding uranium plates, something that they hadn't been able to do before. They did some photo micrographs to see if there were any voids in my work and they were perfect. When they wrote up the report on submerged arc welding on uranium they failed to give me any credit. Duncan, my supervisor, was so upset about my treatment that he actually left the Lab.

"Don Sandstrum came in all gung ho; he was a metallurgical engineer and had a Masters. He said, 'You guys can't do anything until I tell how to do it.' I said, 'Fine, but nothing is getting done.' One day he asked me, 'Ruben, what am I doing wrong?' 'Don, why don't you let the techs do their job. We know the materials. You have all your theories, but we have a feel for the materials, we know what works.' So he took my advice and later told me that that was the best lesson he ever had."

ROBERT DINEGAR—*Weapons Expert/Minister*

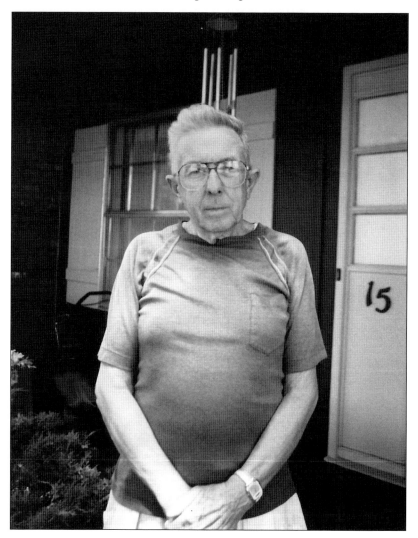

Robert Dinegar

I was on my way to becoming a priest, so I went to Cornell and majored in the classics. The time was late 1940 and war clouds were on the horizon. I spoke with an Army recruiter who told me I would never make it through school, I would be drafted. The Army would never support my religious studies, he said, so if I were you I would switch majors, try something practical like engineering. Then when you go into the service they won't hand you a rifle.

I went on to get a doctorate at Columbia as a student in chemistry. A friend had come out to Los Alamos six months earlier and claimed it was the greatest place in the world. I came out in 1950 and they gave me a choice of working in radioactive material or explosives. I accepted a job in GMZ Division and worked in Group 7 where we made the initiator explosives that were used in atomic weapons. I spent 37 years in the same group. We measured things like detonation velocity.

I had what was called a "renewed vocation" to be a priest. I approached the Episcopal Bishop of New Mexico and he agreed to let me study for five years, then he ordained me to the priesthood. I accepted the call from Trinity on the Hill Episcopal Church in 1959 as their associate pastor and stayed until 1983.

There is sin in the world, always has been, always will be. There are bad actions and these actions must be controlled. Unfortunately, very unfortunately, one of the ways of controlling large-scale improper actions is the work that we do in Los Alamos. Norris Bradbury put it so well when he said, "The purpose of Los Alamos National Laboratory is to keep the world at peace until we learn to live together in harmony." That sums up my theology, my philosophy, and the function of the Lab.

Do you remember the book, *I Led Three Lives*? I've led three lives. I've been a Naval officer, I'm still a priest, and I've been a scientist. I would like to live three lives and have each one of them the main focus of my life, I mean do them separately. I want to live three times, not because I'm the least bit dissatisfied, but I would love to just live three lives in which I do each one of those things only and see what happens.

BEN MAESTAS—*Technician*

Ben Maestas

I was single, just out of the Navy. Being from Colorado, we knew all about the work ethic. When I was hired there were only six Spanish technicians in the whole Lab. I got in because of my work on torpedoes, gyroscopes in particular. I spent quite a bit of time bomb testing in the islands.

There was something called "test effect." I was thinking about it the other day. Who was that guy who blew up the Oklahoma building? Timothy McVeigh referred to the children as "collateral damage." That's what I thought of the soldiers as, collateral damage. They set out monkeys, they set out rats. There was a gal at Highlands who set out the piñons [trees]. They blew up things that looked like hotels.

I was on a shot where they had pigs and medical people on call with ambulances. They had built a five-story building and on each level they placed the pigs. They'd feed all the pigs every day until the big blast. The doctors poured in after the shock wave had passed to see how many of the pigs they could save. They actually performed surgery on many of these poor animals.

I'm glad I took this path. I was loyal and proud of what I was doing. I don't want to brag about my work but I was involved in a lot of important stuff up there. As I look back on the Manhattan Project I have some misgivings about all the lives that were destroyed in Japan. There should have been some other way to end the war.

JOE MASCARENAS—*Environmental Waste*

I worked in recovery [restoring various materials that can be reused] for about ten years and then I transferred to Room 601 making fuel pellets. I helped with plutonium 239, making fuel elements for the reactors. At the same time I was also working with plutonium 238. It was very touchy and I didn't care to work with it. I got out of there in about 18 months.

Plutonium 238 is a very volatile alpha emitter. If we have a hole in a glovebox [a physical barrier to protect the operator from hazardous material, made of stainless steel and 3/8" laminated glass with two glove ports to access the work] or anything, it would spread in no time. It doesn't have the half-life of PU-239 but it is very hot. I worked there for a while and then I was transferred to chemical waste. I helped to develop a counter for counting all the waste that was missing. [When a procedure is done to convert a material from solid to liquid or gas, sometimes minute amounts of the original material is lost. Great efforts are made to reclaim these lost particles, i.e. scraping the walls of the glovebox.]

You get the plutonium hemi shells that they were using for experimental work and you'd clean them real good with alcohol. Then you would take them out of one box, out in the open, and transfer them to another hood with a dome in it. You put heat to the tips and you have a coil that puts heat to the plutonium. Then you shoot some gas on it and it coats and turns into a silver or nickel. Once you do it several thousandths in thickness, you can get that plutonium out in the open and there's no contamination on it. You spin it, then set it down, and you have little spots that didn't get coated, so you shoot those.

I did the hemi shells work on and off for three or four years. It all depended on what they wanted. I did tritium recovery work. Never had any proper training on that either. We went through a process of recovering tritium gas from plutonium that had been in storage.

In the olden days they used to manufacture these weapons and they introduced the tritium into the plutonium and the uranium. First you have the stainless steel outside core, then you have the uranium, and finally the plutonium inside. The tritium had been introduced in order to make the weapon. Since they hadn't used them they were stored. We used to get them from Savannah River [Savannah River National Laboratory of applied research and development], and all over the country. Our job was to recover the tritium.

First you cut it open, O.K? You have to have a good atmosphere because you are in a glovebox. In order to not start plutonium on fire you have to have an argon atmosphere in the box. In those days they didn't have the detectors that they have now. I recall I was taught how to test the atmosphere in a box. You introduce the argon and let it run for four or five hours to get rid of all the oxygen. Now you have an argon atmosphere. But to make sure you do, you try and light a match. If it doesn't light, you have good atmosphere, but if there were other gases in there can you imagine what would happen?

ANTONIO GUILLEN—*Technician*

I think I was 57 years old and I already had 56 Rems [Rem is the basic unit of radiation; 56 is a very high amount]. ACT -12, the people who record the exposures and keep the records, called me, very alarmed, and said, "Tony, we need to get you out of there." They called a meeting and sure enough, the boss said I couldn't go back in. "We can't allow you to go near radiation anymore." I asked, "What am I going to be doing?" "From here on in, Tony, it's TLC for you." Three weeks later they came to me and said, "We re-calculated your numbers and you're O.K. to go back in."

You question this kind of thing but what can you do? You still don't want to refuse them so close to retirement, about three years. I couldn't risk it; I might lose everything. I had worked on metal and then I transferred to aqueous solution. What you do there is separate plutonium from any possible contaminants it has—any kind of trash, gloves, ceramics, whatever. I was recovering plutonium with an ion exchange, nitric acid. Later I moved to another operation where I used hydrochloric acid.

HAROLD ARCHULETA—*Plutonium Specialist*

To do one job, like a shell casting [filling a mold, in the shape of a half sphere, with molten plutonium or other metals], it could take all day because it has to be perfect. An ingot [a mold in which a metal is cast] might take a couple of hours. On the ingot, once everything is set, you have your water connected, everything going, you go to your instrument panel, hit a button, and it starts pulling vacuum on it. You watch the gauge and see the needle climbing. Once you get to the right level, you would close your valve and open another one and your vacuum would settle down to zero. Then you knew you had good vacuum. If it stayed about fifty, your vacuum wasn't any good. So you would have to take it all apart, break your seal, unscrew and lift the lid up. There might be some debris or something that is creating the leak. It takes a while, and all this time you're there in front of the glovebox and your count is building up because of the plutonium that's close by. You have dosimeters, film badges, to tell you how much you're picking up.

If it's a rush job, then you can get someone to help you. But there are not that many trained to do that job. There were only two or three of us doing the casting. If they were busy, it's up to you to finish the job.

Once you stirred enough depending on which alloys were used, you let it sit a while and let all the debris come up to the top. All this cruddy stuff rises and leaves the pure metal at the bottom. You are up on a ladder, viewing this from the top of the box. You have to get up top where there is another set of gloves and you put pressure on the stopper rod just in case. Plutonium has a tendency to get under the plug and lift it up. So you are applying constant pressure. All this time, all this radiation is hitting you right in the stomach, and from the stomach down. Once you think everything is homogeneous, you're ready to pour, let it sit twenty minutes and then pull the plug. Once you pull the plug you can get down and come over to where there is a little window on the bottom. You can see the bead going straight down, bright red. Plutonium melts at 640 degrees centigrade. You have to take the temperature up to about 900 degrees. The crucible is bright red, the metal inside is bright red and you can feel the heat on the window. The gloves get hot and you can see the straight line going down into the crucible. Once it stops that's it. You go turn your power off and you let it sit and cool down. Wait a couple of hours. Then you have to unload it. You turn off your vacuum, close the valves, break the vacuum seal, take off the lid, and remove the glass. Make sure you don't bang it, break it, and cut yourself. Put it away on the side. Remove the crucible out of the coil, move the coil out of the way because it would swing off to one side. Lift the small lid, not the whole thing, and pull your crucible out. The crucible is tied together with an aeroseal clamp. Unscrew it, pry it open, and there's your ingot.

Then you have to weigh it. Get your casting card and enter the weight of the ingot. Maybe you started with 3,500 grams and the ingot might weigh 2 kilos. You then knock out what remains inside the crucible, the "skull" we would call it. You have to get it out and weigh it. You have to balance out and that's hard to do! A lot of the fumes come out and they get on the glass tube, so you have to scrape the tube. Once you gather up all these tiny amounts, you have to burn it, oxidize it. Then you weigh the oxide. So you enter the weight of your ingot, your oxide, and maybe you are still ten grams short. Where did they go? You look around, you wipe the place clean and a little will stay in the rags. The rags have to be examined too. After all this it usually balances out, but sometimes it doesn't.

Nobody handled more plutonium than we did in Los Alamos. In the old days before TA-55 [plutonium facility, for a good ten years it was pretty busy. In fact we used to work Tuesday and Thursday nights until 9:00 p.m. overtime. We had so much work that we even went in on Saturdays. We worked and worked and then moved to TA-55 and after about ten years it started to slow down. The Tiger Team came in [see Manny Trujillo and Joe Gutierrez] and that was it, everything went to pot.

CHARLES MILLS—*Pro Force (Security Guards)*

There were about 100 men in the class. We went through the training, which was basically a police course. The head of the security force was a man named Col. John Carroll. He had come from Massachusetts and had been connected with the State Police there. So we ended up getting more police training. But we also had a judo class and threw each other over our shoulders and all like that. I got to be thinking, if those people where we are going to be working in Los Alamos need to be handled like this, that's really gonna be a tough job! But anyway, it went on and we got through it. They had really nice snappy uniforms. Had that western Stetson hat and we had black, shiny jump boots. You could attract attention wherever you went. When we finished training, we all came in convoy through Santa Fe. I was surprised at how small it was. I had heard about it all my life. I expected it to be bigger. We came right down to the old Capitol Building and then they took us through Burro Alley. Came on down and then we saw this rock out on the road that looked like a camel—Camel Rock. Then we came across the old suspension bridge at Otowi [across the Rio Grande]. It was just one way and the trucks couldn't make it. They had to go around by Española. It looked like awfully rough and rugged country coming on up the hill.

One of the more interesting things to me was, when spring came and the pistol range was thawed out and the snow melted, I began to go and shoot a lot. Our range master was George Irwin. I would go out there just about every day after work. He'd issue me any amount of ammunition that I wanted to shoot. That's what I liked—you could get all that free ammunition if you wanted to build up your skills. There were a few others who practiced a lot. Finally, in early summer, George Irwin got permission from Col. Carroll to form a pistol team of the four best pistol shots. That included George Irwin, Orville Burnworth, a man named Bullard, and myself. We ended up as the Force's Pistol Team.

Phil Schofield [a technician with a wide range of working environments at the Lab over a twenty-year period], who grew up in Los Alamos, told me, "We used to sneak out to the old rifle range, which is behind Guaje Cemetery. Those hills they used to use for backstops are so filled with lead, tons of lead there. We would sneak back there, take a spoon with us, and dig up the old bullets. We would bring the bullets home, melt them to get the lead, and make fishing weights and shot material for slingshots."

We shot one match with the State Police. Four of them came up and we had a little informal match out at the range, and another time or two like that. Then they said that we could go to the NRA-sponsored regional matches in Denver. We would represent the Security Service. They would furnish us transportation, that is a Buick Road Master sedan. They would pay us our wages but we had to furnish our own lodging and meals. It cost us a little bit but we were anxious to take advantage of it, I'll tell you.

So we went up there, and that was the first pistol match I was ever in. We did pretty good. We won some medals to bring back to show Colonel Carroll what we had accomplished. He was quite pleased with it. He liked the publicity, good publicity, wherever he could find it. So the four of us stayed on the team for the year of 1948. Finally, there were others who got good enough to form a second four-man team. So after that, when we went to matches we'd take two four-man teams. We remained team number one because, if I do say so myself, we were a little better than anybody else around here.

I'll tell you an interesting part of the security work here was accompanying shipments back and forth across the country. Shipments of either classified documents or nuclear materials that had to have a certain amount of protection at all times. One trip that I was on, a crew of eight or ten of us took a load of nuclear material in what they called "bird cages." We accompanied this load down to Albuquerque early in the morning. This was loaded on two old B-29 bombers that they had there at Kirtland Field. They were huge planes and no longer in use by the Air Force.

We took those bird cages and put them in the bomb bay, stacked them in there. Each one of them had a parachute attached to it and the rip cord handle had a piece of line, a rope tied to that which was attached to the inside of the plane. So, we had two planes like that with half our group in each one. The plan was, if one of those planes started down, they especially didn't want something like that to go down and get burned. It would be a great loss, and a danger. In case something went wrong and one of these planes started down, the pilot would jettison those bird cages. He'd open the bomb bay doors and those bird cages would slide out and when it got to the end of the rope, the ripcords would get pulled and the parachutes would be engaged. Of course, we had parachutes too. We were supposed to take a flying leap off that plane, pull the ripcord, and get those things in sight and try and follow them down and guard them once they hit the ground!

I guess there were about eight or ten on each plane. These bird cages with nuclear material, too much mass of it close together could flash. You can only get so much of it close together, so you didn't want these lead pigs [containers for source material] close together. They had a metal framework welded around them with the pig in the center, so they provided the space to keep these apart.

We were taking them to Fort Hood at Killeen, Texas. It was in the spring and the wind was terrific when we took off. We got down there and the plane that I was on had no problems, came in and made the landing All right, but the other one came in and the pilot tilted it up and most of the weight landed on one side. It burned right through the rubber and several layers of cord in those big old huge tires. He managed to land O.K., but he wasn't about to take off again on those tires.

Security men on horseback

DOUG VENABLE—*Physicist*

I've been with the weapons part of the Laboratory ever since I came. You like to know how these things behave with respect to the high explosives squeezing things together. The Germans worried about that, too. One of the ways to observe it was to use x-rays, flash x-rays bulbs. You could look through the high explosives and see what was going on. What had been done here just before I arrived was that the Lab had a contract with a radio firm whose name I won't mention. They were to investigate a design and needed an x-ray machine to do it. One of my tasks was to go as an overseer of what they were doing. These people were made up of escapees from Berkeley Lab where they had done a lot of electron accelerator work. They didn't, however, direct their efforts as I thought they should have. My immediate boss was a chemist, so I had to serve as his eyes and ears for some of this. We had to call their contract to a halt because they weren't doing the job properly. This was about the only time I used my academic background to cross check things.

Then the question was, who's going to do it? Well, I had to do it. So I made the first design of a thing called PHERMEX, a pulsed high energy machine emitting x-rays. It's a flash x-ray bulb with pulses that were two tenths of a microsecond long. It's shorter now. We could stop the motion of these things; stop it in the sense that there would be no motion sphere in that small exposure time. High explosives are driving things at enormous speeds, and you want to stop them. We were very successful doing that. It took us 12 years to get that built.

It was built at R-site. It's all encased in a large, blast proof bunker. I made the first proposals in 1951 and went out to talk to Ernest Lawrence at Berkeley about what we were doing. He was doing a lot of the accelerator work, there at Berkeley. He was very polite, took me out to lunch at the faculty club and did all these nice things. The most interesting thing he did was to tell a few men to go down into the basement, bring up a small accelerator, take it out to the Nevada Test Site, set it up at Sugar Bunker, and try some experiments. They did. They invited me out for this. There was nothing untoward at all. Everyone was above board. I came home. This was the stimulus we needed to get some reluctant people on board for the project. The Director and my boss had already endorsed it. It probably would have gotten done anyway.

When a piece of high explosives squeezes a spherical shell, it squeezes it down to some shape. The density is going to be different throughout that shape. If the shape to begin with is not a shell but a sphere, it still squeezes it. Uranium, for example, flows like water when you squeeze it hard enough. You like to know how it is flowing, how it behaves. That's what the radiography is for. Two chaps, Glen Seed and Leo Perry, both retired from the Laboratory, had done the initial static radiographic work, the x-ray work. They showed how well an x-ray could be used to replicate the density distribution, that is, how dense things are. Instead of being 19 grams per cubic centimeter, it might be 25 when it got really squeezed. So you get different densities, different blackenings on the film. You unfold that and relate that to the mass density in the thing that you are looking at. That was very successful. It's kind of interesting in that nobody has done that ever since.

Cockcroft-Walton accelerator

JACK AEBY—*Photographer/ Health Physics*

Jack Aeby

ON PHOTOGRAPHING TRINITY:

I had on welder's goggles. There was always the chance that the bomb was going to fizzle. I had the aperture of the lens set wide open. I was focused at infinity. It was on bulb, that is, I had my finger holding it down and it was open. It was dark outside, no problem. But if it fizzled, I wanted to get what little light there might be, so I would have held it until it was apparent. I wasn't looking through the viewfinder at this time. I was using the back of a chair as a tripod, hand held on the back of a chair, holding the lens open on bulb. As soon as it went it was obvious that it was not a fizzle, so I released the bulb, cranked the lens opening down to ... I don't even know. Then I shot three rapid shots.

I was using a Perfex 44 camera, a 35 millimeter. It turns out that the middle one of the three shots was about the right exposure. It didn't matter what the aperture really was. I would have taken more pictures but that was the end of the film. Color film was hard to come by in the War and I happened to have a roommate who was head of the photo division. He managed to find a hundred foot roll of Ansco color film.

I was shooting on my own. There were a few professional photographers there; Berlin Brixner was one. You may want to talk to him. He's still alive, I think. He was last week! He was a member of Julian Mack's group that was in charge of the official photography for the Lab. Segre [an elite Italian physicist, recipient of the Nobel Prize] had gotten me security clearance on the basis that he wanted to document his group's activity. I did that and the black and white photos exist. When it came time for the "shot" I switched to the remaining bit of color. The head of the photo division clipped off a chunk of the roll and I loaded it personally into a cartridge and carried it down there.

There was no other color picture made that came out. It was used by the theoretical division to make the early measurements of yield because they could measure where I was, the focal length, and the diameter of the fireball, this kind of thing. And an estimate of what fraction of a second or so after the blast it was shot. It had that importance. I developed these myself. Anscochrome was available for personal use, a home, seven color process. The chemicals were available.

The blast occurred in the morning, and our group left the test site on the same day. We had data that needed to get back. I developed that same night in the laboratory darkroom, the reproduction department's darkroom, which was not official photography, that was in Julian Mack's place. I developed it there, and somebody saw it the next morning hanging in the darkroom. I knew I had a picture when I went home.

ON HEALTH PHYSICS:

That term applies to looking into and checking on the effects of radiation and to watching people to make sure they don't exceed certain levels of exposure. I worked alternately in groups that were simply going with people in those areas and a research group that was trying to measure radiation more accurately. As a result of that, our group did get involved in the testing from then on. If there were any tests between 1946 and 1949, I missed them, but I was on all the tests in the 50s: Redwing, Operation Crossroads.

Our duties on the test sites involved going with recovery groups after shots and setting up monitoring conditions throughout the operations as to rules and procedures to make sure people were wearing film badges, etc. We manned checkpoints to make sure that the right people went to the right places. It was a matter of personal monitoring, to make sure they stayed within the prescribed limits. It started out in the early days at 15 Rems a year; after a while, they dropped it to 5R per year, and now I think we're down to about 3R.

Any number of times people accidently carried contamination into the valley on clothing, shoes, etc. A couple of times I was involved in going around the valley and actually stripping people's homes of rugs, towels, etc. We went through and checked everything they might have contacted during the brief period that the employee had been home with the contaminated clothing.

We rotated people in and out of every day, whoever hadn't exceeded their radiation limits for the period of concern—the quarter or the year. I worked at 10 sites where they prepared these radio lanthanum sources for the shots at Bayo Canyon. That was a highly radioactive area. The job was highly radioactive. Say, if the exposure cut-off was 20, rather than have to write up the report, if I saw a number like 21 or 22, something that I knew was no different than 19, I wouldn't fudge the record but would certainly make some effort to justify lowering it to get it under the cut-off. The politicians and the bureaucrats get in there and you've got two hours of writing reports when you could solve it in a few minutes by simply saying, well, my instrument wasn't functioning right or find some other reason.

I'm not condoning it, but believe me, that's going to happen. I will only justify it up to a point, beyond that I would write the report. It was a personal judgment and in technical work there is no place for that. If it goes over the level, you really should report it and take the consequences. I've been on both sides of the issue. I understand where those levels came from. They are just as arbitrary as can be. Nineteen would be as good as twenty.

ON BOY SCOUTS:

During the war it was very loose in Los Alamos, people would come and go. You knew everybody in town. If there was a party everybody went. It was really a very pleasant experience. I was a young punk rubbing elbows with Nobel Prize winners right and left. I still managed to find time to become the Scout Master and re-start the troop that was with the Ranch School.

We had Vences Gonzales, the old-timer who knew the trails and where to go. The Army was very generous. They would commandeer … 6 and haul us out in the middle of the Valle Grande or La Valle de Las Mosas, dump us off and come back in three days. The last trip I took with the boys was the day the war ended. We were coming back with our horses packed, down into an area just below S-Site and Kistiakowski [a well-known physicist] decided to celebrate the war's end. He set off a bunch of scrap explosives … BAAM. Every time one of these went up the horses took off through the woods, scattering their packs all over the place. We no more got them rounded up than he'd let another one go. We knew that the war was over.

ON THE NEVADA TEST SITE:

The Nevada Test Site was very different than test sites in the islands. I'm trying to recall the sequence of events. The first operation was Buster Jangle. Ahead of that first operation public relations teams went out. I happened to be one of the participants as a health physics representative. There were military people, engineers, and the ones from the test site office. Our job was to go around the perimeter of the test area and talk to community leaders. There would be a meeting set up in each of these small communities. We'd come in with our "dog and pony" show and tell them all about radiation. The most frequent question we got asked was how close to the test site can I put a hot dog stand? These are county officials, city officials, business leaders, and interested citizens and that was the kind of question we got.

LEO VIGIL—*Nuclear Transport*

Leo Vigil

I used to haul all kinds of contaminated stuff, not just pluto-nium. I used to haul what they called a lead pig, which takes a "source" from one laboratory to another. There was one that weighed 22 tons. I remember one time coming from Pajarito site to TA-46, when one of the doors opened. I was riding by myself, so I got down to tie the door down because as heavy as it was it would have broken off if I let it flap. Here comes somebody in a government car that was probably from the Laboratory, and he asked me if I had a walk around going on [what a trucker does to check his load]. I said, sure, I have to tie this thing. All I had was rope, so that's what I used. He started asking if I was one of the 26 who were checked who had more milligrams of plutonium. I think I was one of them, but they never told me flat out. Like I say, we were very naive about these things. We didn't know anything about this stuff and what it could do to you.

I worked there for 38 years. I started at 18, so more of my life was spent in Los Alamos than it was at home. Then we had the underground testing up in Los Alamos before they took it to Nevada. We used to work there 24 hours a day until the government sent word questioning how people could work so hard for so long.

They were doing the same thing here that they were doing in Nevada. We had a site on the road to Bandelier [National Monument] where we'd test them. I was hauling continually around the clock. I remember one time a bunch of radiation came out of one of these holes. I remember a lot of laborers, especially from Chimayó, were exposed—Ernesto Córdova was one, but I can't remember others.

They not only had to check all the workers, they had to go and check their houses, too. It happened to me, but in the CMR Building. We were hauling some hot stuff and they didn't check up because we were in a hurry. They sent us home. I always checked myself when I got to work the next day. That was my routine. The meter went up to the top. Some of those Geiger counters were kind of sensitive, so I thought maybe I'm touching it wrong. I called one of the guys from the Press Building next to Sigma to come and check me. I said, "What do you think?" He said, "I think you're hot. Where have you been?" "I've been home. This is the first job of the day." I told them they had to come and check my house, my car, and at first they refused. They said that it was a lot of paperwork and this and that, and I said, I don't care, you are going to check my house regardless. Finally they sent Alfred Fernandez, one of the decontaminators. He died four or five years ago. Another guy who worked with him is also dead. Then they sent Manual Salazar because he was

Demolition of D Building, circa 1950. "D Building was the plutonium facility located at Ashley Pond and considered one of the
most contaminated in the whole Lab. When they built new buildings across the canyon it was our job to haul off the demolished D
Building. The carpenters cut it into pieces and I loaded sections
onto my 40-foot trailer, wrapped it in tarps and hauled it to the hot
dump. We had pressurized suits because it was so hot. We had to
bathe 4 or 5 times a day just being around the site. When we were
ready to haul a load we hosed down our tires so as not to contaminate the roads."—Leo Vigil

Demolition of D building

with the AEC [Atomic Energy Commission] and would assess damages. They went through and found some contamination on the sofa but couldn't get it out with masking tape. They tried and they checked and said it was all right, but I still wondered. Later that same day they took all my clothes off and put me in coveralls. After that I used to get a lot of rashes every time I'd be in contaminated areas. I used to tell the doctor at my routine check-ups every four or five years, you know what, you check me for radiation. The doctor's name was Flint and we nicknamed him "big finger" Flint. He told me that it was up in my head. I said, "It's not in my head, it's all over my leg." He said, "What do you know about radiation?" I said, "I think I know more about it than you because I have worked with it for many years. You're just a company doctor and you don't care what you tell me. You know what? They pay you to lie, you're just like the rest." He said, "A little baby oil will take care of it."

REFLECTIONS ON THE LAB:

We were the ones that stopped the war but look at how many innocent people it took to do it. Of course, they killed a lot of us. If I had to have my work life to do over again, I would never be involved in anything having to do with war. I hate the killing. What does the first commandment tell us? Thou shalt not kill! Oh, I'm such a good Christian. What kind of a Christian kills, for whatever reason?

Jobs have always been scarce here and we jumped at them. We really had no idea what we were getting into. It was a good government job that paid better than most. The second generation up there, they have good jobs. They know what we created and they go in with their eyes open. They may even be doing creative work that doesn't involve weapons. When you create something to go kill your neighbor, I don't think that's right.

CHARLES KELLER—*Astrophysicist*

I got interested in astrophysics so I went and got my doctorate at Indiana University. They had a strong connection with one of the groups at Los Alamos. That group did computer modeling of things that were involved with radiation from starlight and flow dynamics. I did my thesis as a student on computer models of stars that pulsate. They get bigger and smaller, brighter and fainter. The first variables were discovered in Cepheus (Cassiopeia's husband). You can tell how far away everything is by looking at them because the time it takes for them to pulsate is related to how bright they are. You can calculate distance.

We got involved with security modeling. As an example, somebody sets off some kind of nerve gas in a city and we can track it. There are two ways to do that, one to see it, or develop sensors to see it and follow it. Then give it to the computer models and project where it is going. Who has the best forest fire model in the world? Los Alamos. We have a computer model that will follow a fire precisely where it goes. In fact, just before the Cerro Grande fire [in 2000], a computer simulation was done to see what would happen if a fire started at the back corner of the Lab. It turned out that when it got to the Lab that's exactly where it started. These computer models are now being used by the Forest Service.

We have two of the best ocean models in the world. One came from the University of Miami and the other from the Naval Research Lab. They came to interact with our group of experts in fluid dynamics and modeling in general. The ocean is fluid. If you blow on it you make currents, but the earth is spinning so that changes the way the flow goes. If the water gets cold and dense, it'll sink. If it warms it will rise: buoyancy. The Los Alamos Lab now has the model, which has been selected by the National Science Foundation for the national climate code. Los Alamos has always been good at moving things, fluids and turbulence from the beginning to the end. So we were worrying about water resources, atmospheres, oceans, earthquakes. We were modeling things like how does the earth make its magnetic field.

The history of my life at the Laboratory is that of a gradual opening up and doing more and more. Look at the work we have done on the human genome. Fantastic! But these people stick you with a role. I remember Sig Hecker [Lab Director from 1986 to 1997] was speaking to the Buchbaum Committee. They asked what the Lab did and he said, a lot of non-defense work. They asked, what was his major role? He said it was defense. You can't claim your role is defense when you are doing all this other non-defense work. Sig had to come back and re-character-ize Stockpile Stewardship [the program that works to make sure existing weapons are viable] to keep the Lab running. So the question remains, how do you do both and still justify yourself in the minds of the politicians? I remember asking the Deputy Director, is there a place for people to work at the Lab who don't care at all about defense? He said, "That sort of sounds good, but we really are all about defense." I maintain that half of the really smart people in the United States are just not available to the Lab because it always says that whatever we do should help in defense. It sort of scares these people away.

PAUL MONTOYA—*Technician*

On March 7th of 1942, the United States passed an act of Congress to condemn all these lands in Los Alamos for what they called the "demolition range." We had 160 acres with cat-tle on it. It was right next to what was called Anchor Ranch. In 1942 I was seven years old and everybody was gone to war at that time. My dad was working in the shipyards of California. We were out there, one summer in July of 1943: my grandfa-ther, José Montoya, my dad's father, who was 72 years old at that time, my brother Gilbert who was 11 years old, my cousin Joe who was 13, and I, who was seven, were tending to the animals.

At those times we all worked, pitched in on the farm.

Ten U.S. Marshals came out there in military jeeps and they forced us off our lands at gunpoint. They told us that the federal government had taken over and then escorted us down to where the water tanks are, about 14 miles. They escorted us right through that deep canyon by the hospital. There was no bridge out there then. We had horse wagons and lost about eighty head of cattle, which we couldn't take out.

They told us that we couldn't take anything. We had to leave immediately. They took us out about nine o'clock and took us down to the water tanks, right through Los Alamos. They were behind us all of the way with guns drawn. They told us flatly that they would shoot at us … they were under orders.

We actually thought that they were the enemy taking us out, you know. We knew that there was a war going on. We thought they were probably German or Japanese taking us out. They left us out there where the San Ildefonso Reservation starts. They knew that we were living there and they probably thought that we were tribal members. That's probably why they left us there. They wouldn't treat them that way today.

I ended up working for the Lab. When I first started at TA-1 there were about 25 technicians who had been left behind to clean up all the powder metallurgy. They had so much junk, so many cans of what not, so what they decided to do was to dig a trench out there. It was maybe 200 feet long and 30 feet wide and 20 to 30 feet deep. Some of those trenches are out there from TA-55 on down. They are on that side of the road, on the north side of the highway. I don't know, maybe they moved the highway now.

I had been working out there about a year and my boss came up to me and said, "By the way, we are going to get rid of all these jars and we don't know what they are." We had a meeting and they told me to just get rid of them, go ahead and grab the little government truck and we'll load as many jars as we can. We loaded maybe two hundred. He says, "Go out there where there's a trench but make sure that they all break. We don't want the bulldozer to run over them and get blown up." So I said, "O.K." and went out there and pitched in the first one and had a big explosion!

Nobody knew what was in the jars and nobody wanted to deal with it. So I exploded a whole bunch of them. Then I went back and told all the fellows. By that time they had borrowed some other pick-up trucks. They had jars, I don't know, four or five thousand of them to get rid of, some pints, mainly quarts, all pretty well sealed. So pretty soon we started having a contest. By this time we were six or seven guys. We tried to see who could get the biggest explosion. They go up 20 or 30 feet. We kept pitching those jars … it must have taken us almost two weeks to finish the job. We had to break every one. If one failed to break we had to pitch rocks on it until it did. Some were duds. We got that whole area clean and it so happened that we had to get on our knees and crawl under a building. There were plumbing fittings there, many that looked new, but nobody dared take them. We cleaned the whole area out and then moved on to the other building.

RICKY ORTEGA—*Painter*

I started at TA-55. It was under construction, union work. Then I got laid off and I was still in the union and they called me back for Zia [a private contractor]. I started as an apprentice and did my four years and then moved on to journeyman.

TA-55 is on the highway that goes between Los Alamos and White Rock. Everything has changed so much now. At that time it was under construction but most of it was done. They were already laying off the new guys and letting the old ones stay. I made it about six months there. I was spraying plasite [a material that was sprayed on floors and walls in an attempt to create a barrier from radiation] like concrete, grey in color. It was sprayed real heavy and then troweled to fill in all the honeycomb. The walls were solid concrete, pitted in some areas. We applied just the interior. We would work down the long walls while the trowel men would follow and then we'd check that all small holes and cracks were totally sealed.

The building was three stories and very large. In six months we didn't come near to completing it. They had a crew in the morning, then at 4:30 p.m. another would relieve them. We were all doing the same job, shooting the plasite.

We used to use an airless sprayer called a Bulldog. That thing had so much pressure it was like shooting a 357 Magnum. Sometimes we would change off because the sprayer would get worn out. You had to rotate. The stuff was so strong that it would paralyze your lungs, you couldn't even talk. They had a lot of blowers, which helped to a certain extent. There was another kind of plasite they used for the finish coat, which was even stronger. I used it in DP West later on. I was young and I didn't give a damn about safety, although I would respect the sign or the red light that was on, or whatever. I went back to T-55 later after everything was done.

From 1977 to 81 I did a lot of fiberglass work. They would build something like a house and would put all their containers inside, and we would have to seal them with fiberglass. They would take them to the "hot dump." These containers were about 20 x 30, the large ones. I never saw what they put inside, but I did spray 55-gallon drums another time. We sprayed them with a kind of grease. The tractor would come and take them away, I don't know where. Then they would bring us another container and we would do it all over again.

The worst part of what I did was that I had to spray some tunnels under DP West. They were about five feet by four feet at the most. Pipes ran through there. We had to use all kinds of paints to control the contamination. I used a full face mask with air filters, and we had to remove our clothes and put on three pairs of coveralls including a plastic pair, and three pairs of rubber gloves. We would stay in for two hours and then get pulled out. Then another two, three guys would go in, and on like that. I would work with certain painters and then not see them for months at a time. It was a big operation.

When we came out they would take off our clothes real carefully, and another guy would set us up with new clothes and send us straight to the shower. We would then be checked again. I would go into the tunnel maybe three times a day. I stayed there about a month and a half. They changed me back to fiberglass after that.

PHIL SCHOFIELD—*Technician*

Phil Schofield

I started out in what was called the carbide program, out there at DP [D Plant at TA- 21]. In the carbide program we were taking depleted uranium oxide, plutonium oxide, and carbon and we were making a blend out of it. We were making fuel pellets for the breeder reactor up in Richland, Washington. These were experimental fuel cell loadings where we made what we called pins. The originals pins were approximately a meter long, the same as fuel rods. What we would do is make plutonium carbide pellets in the middle, and there would be some depleted uranium pellets at either end. In a breeder reactor, in essence, what happens is like when you start out with twenty gallons of gas here in Española. You add five gallons of water to your gas. That water had been converted to gas during your trip. So by the time you get to Las Cruces you have twenty-five gallons of raw gas that has to be refined. This is how the breeder reactor works.

Initially, we would take "buttons" of plutonium. We had a carbon arc furnace. We would put them in and basically work two big electrodes. You'd sit there and flip that thing and what you'd do is create a big electrical short. It would cause it to catch on fire and become oxide. It would burn, plutonium will burn, and turn to powder.

We were in Building 150, in gloveboxes. The way it was set up was we had one room where we had some guys doing some special work with assay [determine the quality of the metals involved] instruments and electron microscopes. That was Kay Johnson's section. In the rest of the building we had two projects going. We had the carbide program that was working with plutonium 239 and the other part of the room was devoted to guys making heat sources out of PU 238. They would mostly make little slugs of little balls of spheres. There was one they used to call Senator's ball. It was about the size of a golf ball, a 100-thermo watt source. It looked like a little chunk of black charcoal. They'd keep it in a little crucible and when the big shots came through they'd show it off. When they pulled it off its stand, it was glowing cherry red. It was that hot.

You can't make a bomb out of this stuff, you'd melt down the bomb casing before you could reach a critical mass. But it is a good thing for satellites. You've heard of Cassini [planetary space exploration]? That's what it is, instead of these big 100-watt bulbs, they make these little tiny sources to power the satellites. They're just little bitty things. They're double encapsulated.

We shared space with the 238 guys doing the heat source and I considered what they were handling a lot nastier than what we were doing. And this was back before we had the luxuries of monitoring. That's one of the reasons that they built TA-55, because of the lack of safety, of ventilation. As a matter of fact, we were down in the basement of 150. We were building a new line to do some production down there. We spent about a year building it when they told us to tear it all out. They were going to ship it all out to 55, which was still under construction.

Next, I went to work at 55 in pyro-chemistry. We did a number of different processes. We had direct oxide reduction where you took oxide and reduced it to metal. We had HF [hydrogen fluoride] reduction, which was the same thing only using HF gas. We did salt stripping where we tried to get all the left over plutonium out of the salt. We used calcium chloride salts and calcium fluoride salts. We had electro-refining where we purified plutonium metal. We took it from an impure state and purified it to 99.999%. This was all in gloveboxes. We did a lot of americium extractions, where we would remove the americium from the plutonium metal by means of pyro-chemical processes.

When I say pyro-chemistry, most of this is done at about 800 to 900 degree centigrade. We're using molten metals and salts. When I first started in this work in the mid-80s you'd do all these processes if you worked in the room. You might be doing one thing, one day, and have to help somebody on something else the next. The HF reduction was a very high neutron. It was basically production line assembly at the time I started. We were producing plutonium for Rocky Flats.

They still weren't very concerned about exposures. It wasn't until after the Tiger Teams under Admiral Rickover in the Bush administration, in response to all the problems they were having at Rocky Flats, when the attitude seemed to change. A lot of it was lip service, though. I think a lot of what was initially put in place actually increased exposures because you had so many stupid hoops to jump through to get things done. In the long run,

I think it made us much more aware of the hazards and made the penalties for screw up more severe. But it also made work much, much slower. Very frustrating in that respect, but a positive step from the health and safety standpoint. Now, if there's skin contamination it's reportable to headquarters, not ignored like before.

Too many of the records are gone and too many are bogus. Like I told you, it wasn't until the mid 80s that they all of a sudden starting tracking your exposures. But even then they were fudging. Here's an example. At 55, if you worked on electro-refining you'd wear a film badge for gamma radiation. If you worked on HF reduction, your film badge was designed more for neutron exposure. But, maybe someone was sick that week, maybe someone was short, so you'd be switched over to the other process to help out for a few days or weeks. They wouldn't bother changing your badge. Effectively what happened, if you were on that other process, your exposure wasn't true. I know the Lab would deny this to its dying day, but I know a fudge factor was going on.

What they would do, they would hang dosimeters one meter from the gloveboxes. That was considered background radiation. What they would do is take those readings and subtract that from film badges because that was considered background. But that's not true. Every bit of exposure that you received, you received. It was a numbers game and I saw it played in other areas. Say, someone got … well 5R [Rem] at one time was the limit. If someone went over 5R it had to be reported to Washington. But if they had 4.98 it wasn't a problem. We also wore dosimeter finger rings, which you could get up to 75R on, much more than on the body. If you got 74.9 for the year, it wasn't reported. Most people at 55 wore them. I never saw them at DP. When I had those burns, I know there was some fudging that went on that month. I was right under the limit on both my film badge and my finger ring. On the finger ring, you couldn't get more than 25R in a month.

Alfonso Vargas at PF-4 doing a direct oxide reduction in a glovebox.

Row of gloveboxes

I don't know how they determine the levels—5R whole body, 75R on the hands. It later came down to 50R. I know that one month I was fudged. I had very, very high reading on my hands and on my film badge. But I was just under the limit where it would have been reported to D.C. I had almost 25R for the month on my finger rings, I had 24.95 or some ridiculous number.

If you got close to your annual limit they would put you in a process with lower levels. In some cases, if you were too close to your limit, particularly near the end of the year, they would yank you out of the plant entirely and put you in a cold area with no exposure. They didn't like to have it reported.

Some of my health problems are my skin falls off, and I'm allergic to a whole host of chemicals, perfumes, paints, wood smoke, asphalt, and formaldehyde. Some people call it multiple chemical sensitivity. Some doctors don't believe in it, period. I don't care what name they use, I've been tested and I've got all different kinds of chemicals that I'm allergic to. I get headaches, stuffed up nose, watery eyes, it makes me dopey, and I have trouble breathing. You've seen a sample on my skin—my legs, arms, all turn red. My head swells up, my skin falls off, and I leak like a pine tree.

LYDIA MARTINEZ—*Executive Secretary*

Lydia Martinez

One of my first assignments was at W-1 in Omega Canyon. I worked there for eighteen years as a section secretary. I worked for twenty engineers. We did a lot of classified correspondence. We had to stamp everything, lock our safes, security checks, that kind of thing. From there I went to the Ad Building with Frank Harlow. I did technical reports, work that was unclassified. I learned technical typing which I didn't know before. It was trial and error. At the beginning Frank wrote out the Greek alphabet for me; it was easy, when someone wrote a report you could refer to the alphabet. Later I learned the symbols. I went on to work for George Spielman, a military man, Jim McCleary, who urged me to learn shorthand, and then Frank Carla in T-3. He drove me a little crazy with his paging system—I was part switchboard operator and part secretary. By and large, all my bosses were great. They didn't make you feel that you didn't know enough. They would ask your opinion about the work and I really appreciated that.

On the subject of racial issues, you would see Anglo ladies start working and pretty soon they were group secretaries. Some of them were not competent enough to handle a group office even though they moved up fast. If you go back to the directories, you will not find many Spanish listed. It would have been the division leader, the group leaders, and the secretaries. In those days, you didn't find any Spanish.

There were many local women who could have been group secretaries. There was this one woman who they moved from Oklahoma, with all her furniture, when there were people around here, even within the Lab, who could have taken over the job. But anyway, she didn't like it here. She was used to working for attorneys, so she only lasted a year. They spent more money moving her out. She was replaced by another Anglo.

You know, if Los Alamos wasn't there, it would have been very hard for people here. Having good jobs enabled our children to go to college and now many of them are graduating from big universities. In my family, let's see … on my husband's side there is one who is a chemist on the Hill. The other is an engineer and works for Johnson Control. Two others are lab technicians with degrees in engineering. On my side of the family, my daughter is a pharmacist, my son-in-law is a doctor. Then we have two engineers, a niece and nephew.

If I had to do it all over again I surely would follow the same path. We started from the bottom and I am not ashamed of it. We used to ride the horse to Los Alamos and we had a wagon. I don't see anything wrong in telling people that. Some people have told me I should be proud of how far I have come. I'm not ashamed of the fact that I cleaned houses for the scientists and took care of their kids. And look at all we have. We have our house and three rentals all paid for and our health, which is so important. We're happy and I feel great.

BEN ORTIZ—*Welder*

I hired on in 1969 as a mechanical technician along with many others. This was a time when they were starting the build-up of the linear accelerator at the Clinton P. Anderson facility, known as the Meson Facility. Twenty of us were hired, plus all the personnel already on the project. They needed more man-power—it was a good-sized project.

At the beginning, the duties were varied. Some of the jobs had to do with welding, silver soldering, the washing of many accelerator parts, and a lot of the beam tube, which was stainless steel that was used to make the manifolds. [A beam tube is the main channel where the sub-particles are sent through to their targets. Los Alamos Meson Physics Facility, one of the world's most powerful linear accelerators, opened in 1972.]

Starting in 1969 I began by using a lot of solvents such as trichloroethylene, acetone, and Freon. These solvents had many uses. When we were getting ready with the parts that were going into the accelerator, the first step was to do an abrasive clean on them. If you had the clamshells, you would abrasively clean the side that was to be brazed. [Brazing is an integral part of build-ing the beam tube. One brazes two half-moon shells together, and a stainless steel nozzle is attached to one end. This func-tions to extract unneeded moisture and air in the vacuum-sealed tube].

Then you would go through the process of cleaning them, the wash and the rinse. The wash was the trichloroethylene, the rinse was the Freon. You would actually draw maybe 15 or 20 gallons of each liquid in the baths. They were side by side. They were stored outside the building and they were plumbed in by gravity flow.

You would fill the baths and wash your parts. Of course, there would be splashing that occurred, and the top of the tubs was only plywood. They remained soaking wet most of the time. The floor was concrete and a lot of solvent ran on the floor. The baths were right up against a hood, which was supposed to exhaust the fumes. They never worked properly. Even if they had, I'm convinced they were inadequate.

There were times when we had bridge couplers that provided access to the accelerator. They were about 3.5 feet in length. You couldn't handle them by hand because they weighed quite a few hundred pounds. You used a forklift, which was set almost down to the baths, and then you bucketed the solvent up and over the couplers. So it was all over the place. We also had portable baths of solvent on a different wall of the shop. It was left to just evaporate into the air—there was no drain on these. Knowing what I know today, the practice of safety was never in place. We had face shields for splashes but they weren't completely effective.

The group leader had set up some small pumps underneath the baths. These pumps were supposed to pump out the used solvents back into the empty drums. They were going to recycle it. The stuff is pretty expensive. What happened was the pumps never worked. The next time I was going to wash more parts, I had to bail out the used solvents into a bucket and dump it outside. This went on for quite some time until they decided they were going to do a permanent fix. They hired Zia to dig a trench outside the building. They took it maybe 70 feet to the southeast corner at the end of the pavement and there they dug a pit. That's where the solvents wound up.

There were other things involved with the welding. When you clean out a piece of beam pipe to put a flange on, stainless to stainless, the first thing that you do after you cut it to size and machine it is to wash and rinse it with trichloroethylene and Freon. I found out later that at the time of the welding you're actually making something called phosgene gas. I would get a funny taste in my mouth and lips. I had the welding hood to protect my eyes, but you still get the burn-off from the metal. I suppose if the residue of the solvents was present, I'm not sure what kind of a reaction would be created. It was the same with silver soldering. I used what was called EZ Flow, a silver solder, with a temperature I believe was about 650 to 700. It was used a lot for braising valves, like brass to stainless, and stainless to stainless. I understand that the EZ Flow isn't used anymore because it had cadmium in it, which is very poisonous.

RICHARD CHAPMAN—*Fire Chief*

Richard Chapman

We fought a lot of liquid dump fires. The liquid dump was on DP Road and we would fight those fires with these little respirators. Nowadays you'd have on protective suits and self-contained breathing apparatus. In those days we relied on the Lab management to tell us there was no danger. We'd go in and use water on it to put it out. There must have been some reason why they wanted it out. They didn't want that smoke getting over into the residential area. This was a pit where they dumped all their liquid waste. I'm not sure where the liquid waste came from, but I can almost assume that a lot of it was toxic radiation of one type or another.

There was no medical history taken on people who fought those fires. A monitor would run one over your clothes and if you didn't have any count on your clothing you were OK. They didn't do any swipes of the nose, ears, or mouth. Not only that, but those liquid dumps down around TA-54 on the side of the canyon where they poured liquid and it would catch on fire, we'd flood those things and fill up the pit, and stuff would flow over into the canyons. That's what happened.

It was definitely toxic run-off. Those fires had the most beautiful colors in the world. The only other time I saw those same colors was at the atomic test site in Nevada. I saw the atomic bomb go off and I saw all those colors. There was purple, orange, pink, yellow, and green, all kinds of colors. I saw those same colors in the pit fires as I saw with the A-bomb.

We were fighting a fire over at TA-1 and we went in but we didn't know for sure what we had. The fire was going and we hit it with a stream of water and it exploded. It was being stored in a container of oil of some type and that kept the air from getting to it. When we hit it with that straight stream it removed the oil and the oxygen in the water created the explosion. It went up in the air and when it came down it burned holes in our truck! It was a fifty-five gallon drum full of shavings of material. It was an IUM metal fire of some type, meaning any metal ending in "-ium." Any of these metals will explode when exposed to oxygen, like the aluminum in a Volkswagen. Years back, when the firemen would go in with a straight stream to put out fires in Volkswagen or Volvo engines, all they would get would be sparks.

We used pike poles to keep the oil drums stirred up. What we were doing was cooling them down. They were actually wrecking bars that we stirred with. We were stirring and putting hose streams into them. The water was running over and out. We did this for three or four hours and then they came over and monitored our clothes. We were all hot. We lost all of our clothes, our bunkers [fire department pants, jackets, and boots]. In those days you wore your own clothes, the government didn't furnish them. Most of us wore Levis and a shirt. We lost shoes, socks, underwear, everything.

We also did fire control on experimental explosions. Ancho Canyon was one area. If they figured it was of a certain level of shot, they needed to call us for standby. We'd wait behind a bunker and when it was over the siren would sound and we would go up into the area and check it for spot fires from debris. For instance, if they had red hot metal flying over a large area we'd often find a piece stuck in a pine tree. Whatever it went into, it would set it on fire. Sometimes it would take us an hour, sometimes it would take five hours, and even five days to get it all controlled.

We've had that whole canyon on fire two or three times. It would get up on the plateau on the mesa. We've had fires out at S-site, like the one where they burned waste HE [high explosives]. It was before my time, probably in the late 50s or early 60s. They were dumping HE and what they did was put them on a burning pad and use a squib to light it from a distance. When it's not contained it'll burn up. Just like when you empty a shotgun shell and can light the black powder.

JONATHAN GARCIA—*Area G*

Jonathan Garcia

When I first started with Zia, it was back in 1976, July 8th to be exact. The first day that I hired on they took me to the warehouse where we picked up the scraper, which is an earth mover. The scraper is a heavy equipment machine, a big one, with a belly in the back where you can scrape up the dirt yourself. It had two motors, one in the front and one in the back. You just scrape dirt and fill it up and haul it down into the pits. It is self-loading. You run two different gas pedals, one for the front engine and one for the back. When you start loading, you lift off a little on the front and you push with the back and it pushes you forward. If not it will flip you.

I followed my foreman down to the hot dump. They were digging a pit. That's what I started on the first day, digging pits. They started with the scrapers, three in all, plus a bulldozer with another scraper pulling it. They called it a cat and can. They were old but we used them. We were digging a pit that was 100 feet wide, 600 feet long, and 55 feet deep. It had one real steep entrance, as steep as we could make it and the other side was more gradual because that was where the trucks would come in and dump their loads in the bottom. So that's what I did. I hauled my own dirt every day to bury the material that was brought in during the day from the different areas all around Los Alamos.

They required me to put at least a foot of earth over everything that I was burying, whether it was gloveboxes, barrels, or anything else. We would start at the very end, the steepest side and we would start at the very bottom dumping stuff. When I first started, I would go down there once a week. They would take me and lock me up inside the area. I would start up the dozer, start the scraper, haul my own dirt. By then they would have been hauling in all kinds of junk all week long. It would accumulate, just like in a city dump: trash, anything that came out of radioactive areas. They would call it low-level radiation.

I busted a bunch of the containers and I got contaminated from it. They didn't even have records of when it happened. I hit a cylinder one time, I don't know what it was. The cylinder blew up when I ran over it with the dozer. That's when I first started over there. It picked up the dozer from one side like this and fell back. It was shooting a blaze of fire up into the air—some kind of gas or something. I just dropped the blade, jumped off, left the dozer right there where it was and took off running. I ran all the way to the top of the pit and got in the truck. At that time I had what they called a two man Austin, it was a crane that was set on a truck. That's what I used for transportation down to the hot dump. Thank god that the guy who took care of the area was there, C. O. Martinez. He opened the gate for me and I left. I told him what had happened. Later on my foreman went down there with me. They sent down a monitor because we didn't have one of our own. They checked the dozer and it had picked up quite a lot of radiation. They took me to TA-29 where I showered and showered and was checked several times. Then they let me go, you know. That bulldozer had to be washed with solvents but they couldn't get all the radiation—it was impregnated into the metal.

I ran that dozer for about three or four more years. They said that they had cleaned it. But later on they wanted to sell it and they took it to salvage. They rejected it there because it was still contaminated, even after all those cleanings. So they took it back down to the hot dump and I buried it. I drove it down into the pit and backfilled the whole bulldozer and scraper. I ask questions but they tell me it's low level and not to worry.

That's when I started making noise. I started raising questions as to why we didn't have a monitor there. It was low-level radiation and I was going home with my own clothing. I kept raising hell about it. I felt that I was being lied to, you know. They finally decided to get me shoes. I was wearing white coveralls. I have a picture here. Just regular coveralls and a dust mask, and a little surgical cap, that was it. My regular clothing was worn underneath them.

REBECCA DIVEN—*Technician*

Rebecca Diven

An invitation to work at the secret lab was based solely on the fact that I had trained at Cal Tech in quartz fiber work [microbalance to measure extremely small amounts of plutonium]. I said I would take the job. In due time, a letter came to my boss. He did not give me the letter. He opened the letter, threw the envelope in the trash basket, and read the letter to me. It said that I would need warm clothes, and the usual things that were told to new people, that I would be living in a dormitory and would be eating my meals in a mess hall. The dormitory would cost $15 a month and the mess hall would cost the same. I would be working on a secret project. If I came I could not leave until the end of the war. I would be restricted. I could not have visitors from home. I would not be allowed to leave to go on vacation. I could go to Santa Fe unrestricted. I could go to Albuquerque, I think, unrestricted. But no further than that.

He read me these things and I agreed to them and he left. I then dove into the waste paper basket to see where that envelope came from. I just got it back in as he came back into the room, retrieved it and left. To this day, I think he did it deliberately but maybe not. I saw that the postmark was Santa Fe, New Mexico.

I got off the Super Chief in Santa Fe in a suit. I wanted to make a good first impression. I had on my high heels, my precious nylons, and a perky little hat with a veil. A WAC [Woman's Army Corps] came up to me and asked if I was Becky Bradford [her maiden name]. They looked at me and just shook their heads.

It turned out that these WACs did a little job on the side. Los Alamos had no liquor, so they were doing some rum running. They stopped to get a load prior to picking me up, so they needed to make up some lost time. They chose the old road through San Ildefonso Pueblo and El Rancho, which was off limits because it was so rough and the government-issued tires weren't really up to it. I'm the sole passenger and it rained and snowed like dogs. This road was a sea of mud. Welcome to New Mexico.

After a while we got stuck. They looked at me and said, "We'll help you into the front seat. You drive and we'll push." "But I don't know how to drive!" I said. I had never driven in my life. They looked at me like I was from Mars. "What do we do now, we have a useless passenger." "Well," I said, "I've never driven a car, but I've pushed one before." "In those clothes?" I took off my nylons, and my dainty shoes and put them on the seat. I rolled my skirt up and told them to drive while I pushed. So I did and we clawed our way out of the muck. They said that they needed to make one more unauthorized stop, this time to get me cleaned up before I went for my badge and dorm assignment. That was my introduction to Los Alamos and I made two good friends in the bargain.

I took to life in Los Alamos right away. I liked showers but others resented the fact that they had no bathtubs. We would combine shopping trips to Santa Fe with a chance to bathe. We would take a room at La Fonda and squeeze five of us in there.

I came to the Lab for one thing only, to make a quartz fiber balance. They already had a sizable investment in me. So now I

Stuck in the mud

am going to put all these skills and the jigs together that enable me to make the balance. I am given a separate little room and I create this delicate little thing. But nobody, least of all me, took into consideration static electricity. As soon as you try to weigh something, slam, it went up against the wall of the cage and broke. This took more brains and skill than I had to solve. We got a cage made that kept some of the moisture in to cut this down. I don't quite remember if a chemical was blown in, or a gas, or something. Anyway, they solved the static electricity problem and then came the big day when the division leader and others came and announced that we are going to measure something. It was a little tiny piece of something that went on my tiny little scale and when they took it off they announced we had just weighed the world's supply of plutonium! I became a nervous wreck.

It worked out fine but by the time they got another shipment they had made enough to use a commercial scale. Pretty soon, it was coming through—I use the term loosely—by the ton. Microbalances were no longer needed. So now what do they do with me? I've signed something that said I had to stay for the duration, but you know what, secured away and hidden was a document that said that Becky Bradford may leave the project at the end of her mission. I tore that up and burned it.

So now what do they do with this person who doesn't want to leave? Their solution was to offer me a job in radio assay. They were willing to train me to do it. You have clearance, you have a new job, you like it here, we will train you in this job if you will stay. We would like to have one month to see if you can do the work. You have that same month in which to decide if you like the new job. I had a little lab where I did chemistry to test liquids that came from recovery to see how much plutonium was still in it. I had really good support. They showed me how to do the procedure and they told me what to look for.

RICHARD MONEY—*Chemist*

Richard Money

I started my career as a chemist at Oak Ridge. The laboratory at Oak Ridge had the fullest functioning atomic reactor. So the deal was to produce enough plutonium. They knew that a chain reaction was possible if you had enough fissionable material. That was proven at Stagg Field.

The main job at our facility was to bombard, bombard, bombard U-238, dissolve the bombarded material, and chemically separate the plutonium from all the other fission products. These fission products are the hot stuff that people worry about.

So what we did was work by remote control. You have to take uranium slugs from the pile and you dissolve them. You then go through a chemical process of separating out the plutonium from everything else. It was then sent to Los Alamos. We worked behind concrete barriers between the gamma emitters and us. Our little reactor soon proved inadequate and three large ones were built at Hanford. Why there? Because you had to keep these things cool and the Columbia River was close by. It actually raised the temperature of that mighty river.

The work proceeded in Los Alamos. Periodically we would go in for physical examinations. They found that they couldn't measure our film badges. They were black because we had been exposed to such high levels of radiation. The doctor is reviewing my record and he says, "Dick, you aren't married are you?" I said, "No, I'm not." He said, "Well, if you ever marry with this amount of radiation that you have been exposed to, I doubt very seriously whether you will ever be able to father any children." Since that time I have fathered twelve!

I got to Los Alamos too late to be able to go to Bikini. I stayed in Los Alamos and the samples were shipped from the islands. We were doing the analysis and the work continued for several years. After this work fizzled out we were told a group was needed to do high temperature chemistry. This isn't chemical reactions that occur at 100 or 200 degrees; I'm talking about reactions that take place at 2000 degrees absolute. That's 4000 degrees Farenheit.

Someone got this hot idea to allow a reactor to heat up. Usually the ones that produce power run at about 100 degrees centigrade just to produce water into steam to drive turbines to produce electricity. But suppose a reactor is run at 2000 degrees Celsius; eight hundred degrees Celsius is where steel is made and that's a bright orange color. Go a little higher and the color turns closer and closer to white. Suppose we crank it up to this level and when it's running at this level we have a box made up of fuel elements that have holes running through them. You have a typical rocket design down here. Supposing at high velocity we pump liquid hydrogen, not gaseous, but liquid hydrogen through that box running at 2000 degrees. Can you imagine the specific impulse coming out the rear end of that thing? That was the Rover program. [The Rover project was created to develop a nuclear thermal rocket. Eight reactors were tested between 1959 and 1964: Kiwi, Phoebus, and Peewee.]

I did something in mid-career that was unheard of amongst my peers. I decided to radically change what I did every day for work. We moved into Española (my new wife is Hispanic) and I became a high school teacher—a change of work, a change of social environment, all good things. I maintain my love of Big Band music and continue to play in a band in Los Alamos. I also have my photographic studio and do professional portraiture when time allows. Some have called me a Renaissance man. Could be true.

STEPHANIE SYDORIAK—*Linguist/Homemaker*

I was born in Boston in 1926 to Ukrainian parents. Despite our poverty through the Depression, I managed to attend Northeastern University studying physics and math. I met my husband in a tiny Ukrainian Church. We both studied at Yale. When he got his PhD I had only three months left to complete my Masters, but I didn't think twice. We raced to New Mexico. I liked the idea that Los Alamos personified science and felt confident that I could find meaningful work.

I worked with Virginia Stovall in the microscope section for Louie Rosen. It wasn't my cup of tea, and I developed excruciating headaches staring into microscopes all day long. I was hoping to do some research. No one seemed interested in part-time workers. I already had children to raise at this point. I had a language background and thought there might be a need for translations. I was fluent in French, German, and Russian. I was able to do this work on a more flexible schedule, and I was able to provide this service to the Lab as required.

I spoke to other women who were having similar problems plugging in. Some did pretty well until the first RIF [Reduction in Force]. Women were let go because their husbands were employed and the feeling was that one household should not have two employed in the Lab. One of my friends was let go and she was extremely angry about it. She was eventually rehired but even as a full time worker she felt that women were discriminated against and considered second-class citizens. Her name was Georgia Fritz. She established a group called Women in Science in Los Alamos. Sadly, she died young in a hiking accident but was devoted to receiving equal treatment in the work place.

I eventually gave up on the Lab and turned to music. I put science aside and became a music teacher. My husband suffers from senile dementia and has for the last 12 years. After I had my 6th child I developed myasthenia gravis, which is a muscular weakness. I would be up and down. On down days I would be out, not moving, not walking, not talking, could not lift my arm. I went into remission at 50 and with the aid of medication could lessen the impact of the attacks. As the years have passed I recognize I need more help than the kids can provide.

There are a huge number of Spanish women who work in peoples' homes. There is the more intimate view of what it must have felt like to be from a poor background and come and take care of the well to do. That was very hard for me when I was sick and needed help. I hated the thought of this relationship. That would be telling someone who I consider my equal to do things for me. How would it be perceived by her? I went into spasms about that before I could hire anybody. It was such a dire necessity on my part that I had to. I ended up feeling quite close to these women. My father was a janitor at one point. I have very distinct feelings of how he felt about the rich people he was working for!

As I look back on my life here in Los Alamos, I realize my only real regret is that I never finished my education. Despite that it's been a great place to live and raise my large family. Where else can you live with your doors wide open and never lock your car?

ANTHONY SANCHEZ—*Decontamination*

I was really marriage minded in my early years, but my wife insisted on security. I'll marry you, she said, if you get a job in Los Alamos. So I did that, started as a janitor, then went to the waxing crew, and finally to decon.

There was one room, a pump room that was supposed to be really hot. It was all stainless steel inside. We had to go in and decon it before they started tearing it apart. The deconners and custodians worked together in shifts. One hour and out. After we deconned it to a certain degree, we realized that the concrete floor, which was two feet thick, was contaminated. They brought in some special equipment to cut through the concrete and remove it all. It was like water and sand, the pressure cut through the concrete and rebar too. While they were cutting on top, we were in the basement. We had to shovel all the sandblasted debris into drums and pick up the water, too.

At lunchtime everyone takes off their coveralls at the exit of PF-4 to the main building. They check you out and if you are O.K. you go out to lunch. Well, this went on for several years and then we were told that after everyone finishes lunch, you guys go back in the lunch room, try not to be noticed, and decon the tables and chairs. So they were finding counts on the table.

You know, where we were all eating. You drop a chip on the table and you pick it up and eat it.

So we would go in after lunch and wipe the tables down with Fantastic and cheesecloth, then the RCT would come in and take swipes off the tables and see how they were. They tried hard to keep it quiet but I imagine most knew that it was going on. This was all done after lunch, not before.

I worked in decon from 1986 to1992 and decided sometime after this to leave the job. I left because of personnel issues, the way people were up there, the way I got treated. Also, the training started getting pretty rough. I had a high school education and they were training us with college degree people. They expected us to keep up and it was getting very stressful. I started to bring my problems home. The personnel were real jerks. I hate to say it but it was mainly the Spanish people. Ask anybody, they'll tell you. The day I quit my wife told me, "I was waiting for you to do just that."

I'll tell you the Anglo bosses up there were the ones that treated me the best. After I worked at TA-50 for a while, they were the ones who asked me if I wanted to go with the Lab. I joined, but once I did I noticed a lot of jealousy with the Hispanics. They did everything they could to pull me down. They couldn't see anyone go higher than themselves. I tried transferring to another area, but that didn't pan out. I finally managed to get back into the union and landed a steady job off the Hill. Everything worked out for the best, stress free.

I talk to a lot of men who work up there but they don't like it much. They can't leave because they are in debt. They are locked in. The money is great so they borrow a bunch more to build nice houses, boats, fancy trucks. Then they are all stressed about the bills and the lifestyle they are chained to.

I'm no saint, but I get a feeling that man, Satan sure is dancing up there in Los Alamos.

ED GROTHUS—*Machinist, Activist*

Ed Grothus

I arrived in Los Alamos March 23, 1949. I worked as a machinist in C Shop for 18 months. We did the hydro-dynamics of implosion. They put a phenolic, a plastic dome called a pin dome, right in the dead center of a test bomb. That dome had steel wires coming out of it and those wires had to be in exact positions. You had to know the exact length of them as well. So I'm measuring the wires and positioning the pins where they want them; other people made the pin domes, I did the measuring. Each of these wires came out of the pin dome and went to a pulse-forming network with resistors and capacitors.

The fission bomb consists of a critical mass, plutonium or a fissionable isotope of uranium, right in the heart of the bomb. Then there is a slight gap, a tamper of U-238, and then a pusher, generally of aluminum or beryllium. Then there's the high explosive system on the outside. The high explosives were shaped charges just like the shapes on a soccer ball. On a soccer ball you have hexagons and pentagons, so you only have to make up those two shapes. You need 20 hexagons and 12 pentagons to make up a sphere. They all fit against the pusher.

I quit my job at R- site December 1, 1969. The Vietnam War was raging and that changed my life. We had a group called the Los Alamos Citizens for Peace in Vietnam and I became quite active. I was also an alternate delegate for Eugene McCarthy to the Democratic Convention in 1968.

Some years later when I had established the "Black Hole" salvage company, I decided to send a playful can of soup to then President Clinton. I said in my cover letter that if you eat this you will walk with a halo. If you give some to Socks [the Clinton cat], he'll glow too. Well, they took it as some kind of a threat. This was a can of "organic plutonium." The label tells you it's fat free, wheat free, dairy free, from the reactors of Los Alamos, the home of the A-bomb, grade A approved by the AEC [Atomic Energy Commission] for quality assurance. Distributed by the Primordial Soup Co. of Santa Fe. It was an 8-ounce can of corn, a corny joke.

Anyway, they sicked the Secret Service of Albuquerque on me. They called and came up to see me only hours later. They checked me out and asked if there was insanity in my family. They took handwriting samples and finally concluded that I wasn't a threat to national security.

I am outspoken about my anti-nuclear beliefs but I don't feel intimidated. There are probably people in the Lab who agree with me but dare not express it. I have described over many years the make-up of Los Alamos and the kind of people who have come here. I describe it as being thrice screened. First of all is the self-screening. If you don't believe in the nuclear industry then you don't belong here. Secondly, you have to be a scientist, a physicist, a mathematician, an engineer, or a chemist, some kind of highly trained person. These are good people, smart people, but the fact of the matter is this concentration on science ignores the liberal arts, philosophers, historians, economists. Thirdly, if you decide to come here and are offered a position, you have to have a clearance. They call it a Q clearance, I call it a Q Klux clearance. Understand, they are equal opportunity destroyers, oops, employers. They don't discriminate, but when they check you out, if you have read the wrong books, or belonged to the wrong organizations, or been in a protest rally, they just find a more qualified candidate. So Los Alamos is thrice screened.

[Editor's Note]: The sidewalk in front of the "Black Hole" was in bad shape, so the city decided to repair it. They removed all the cracked cement and poured a new slab. Ed couldn't resist putting his own stamp on it, so he came out in the evening and scratched a peace symbol in the wet cement. It was over a week before the city was informed about what Ed did. They sent out another crew and jack hammered up the entire sidewalk.

Chapter Three

BOMB TESTING

The first test of the atomic bomb, called Trinity, exploded in the New Mexico desert in Jornada del Muerto [Journey of the Dead Man] now part of the White Sands Missile Range, on July 16, 1945. It was the same design as Fat Man, the bomb dropped on Nagasaki, Japan, three weeks later on August 9, the equivalent of 21,000 tons of TNT. J. Robert Oppenheimer was at the Trinity site, but few of the people who were interviewed in this project witnessed the event. Many of them, however, were involved in the hundreds of subsequent tests in the Marshall Islands and the Nevada Test Site.

Between June 30, 1946 and August 18, 1958, the U.S. conducted 67 atmospheric nuclear tests on the 29 low-lying atolls and five islands that make up the Marshall Islands. The islands cover an area of 357,000 square miles north of the equator in the Pacific Ocean in a geographic area called Micronesia. The first tests, called Operation Crossroads, were conducted on the Bikini Atoll, whose 167 residents were persuaded to leave by the U.S. military commander. The object was to test the effect of nuclear fallout on military targets. The first of the tests, called Able, was detonated 158 meters above the target area and sunk the five obsolete ships that were stationed in the lagoon with various animals aboard. The army actually expected more damage but the bomb was dropped off target. The second test, called Baker, was exploded underneath the lagoon water and sunk eight more ships. The fallout from this test stayed largely in the vicinity of Bikini Atoll.

The military moved its testing to the Eniwetok Atoll, where 43 nuclear tests were conducted from 1948 to 1958. Its inhabitants were relocated, some against their will, to Ujelang Atoll. Operation Sandstone conducted three atmospheric tests in 1948 and Operation Greenhouse an additional four in 1951. The first hydrogen bomb, called Ivy Mike, was exploded there in 1952 and vaporized the islet of Elugelab, leaving behind a crater approximately one kilometer in diameter. During that test the military used B-17 bomber drones to fly through the radioactive cloud to accumulate samples for testing. This is what Paul Guthals talks about in his interview.

In 1954 the military went back to Bikini to conduct Operation Castle, which consisted of six surface blasts. The most devastating of these was Bravo, detonated on March first, leaving a huge crater in the reef and vaporizing three small islets. It unleashed greater than expected radiation that was blown by the wind across three nearby inhabited atolls and a Japanese fishing vessel, where one of the fishermen died. The Bikini Atoll was completely contaminated. The story of the native inhabitants of the atolls is heartbreaking: their relocation to smaller islands that failed to provide necessary food and shelter, their subsequent return, a 1975 lawsuit to terminate the resettlement until a satisfactory and comprehensive radiological survey could be carried out, and their eventual abandonment of the atoll in 1978.

Operation Redwing, in 1956, took place on both Bikini and Eniwetok, where so-called "second generation" or more advanced nuclear bombs were tested. Finally, in 1958, Operation Hardtack, a series of 35 tests within the Marshall Islands territory, 10 of them on Bikini Atoll, ended testing in these Pacific Proving Grounds.

The Nevada Test Site, 65 miles north of Las Vegas, was approved by President Harry Truman as a nuclear proving ground

The Bikini Tests, 1946. The operation was to be in 3 shots: the first under water; a surface shot; and an air drop. They organized a fleet of mainly captured German and Japanese vessels. The target vessel was the Japanese command ship, the Yokohama.

in December of 1950. Between 1951 and 1963 the military test-ed 100 atmospheric bombs there (921 underground detonations took place until 1992). The first series of tests called Ranger were conducted in 1951 to test nuclear devices designed at Los Alamos National Laboratory and dropped from bombers out of Kirtland Air Force Base in Albuquerque. Buster-Jangle, the next series, involved thousands of military personnel from all service branches who were stationed at Camp Desert Rock outside of the test site town of Mercury. They witnessed the detonations from trenches and marched towards ground zero after the ex-plosions to collect radiation effects information.

The test called Annie, part of the Upshot-Knothole series, was designed to measure potential impacts on citizens in surround-ing communities. Two houses, filled with food, furniture, and mannequins, were built 3,500 and 7,500 feet from the Yucca Flat ground zero where the sixteen kiloton bomb was detonated from a 300 foot tower. Underground shelters at various distances from the blast were also filled with mannequins. The Encore test tried to determine the impact of an atomic attack on a forest—ponderosa pines were brought to the site—and the Harry test, later dubbed "Dirty Harry," produced the highest level of off-site contamination of any continental U.S. test. All of the tests in this series may have been responsible for one-quarter of all radiation exposure due to the Nevada testing. As is evident in the testimony of those interviewed, many workers and military veterans suffered numerous diseases and after effects from this contamination. After many lawsuits were filed, by not only work-ers but people in the downwind communities, the government was forced to establish compensation programs.

As Ben Maestas talks about in his interview, the government experimented with mice, dogs, and pigs to determine the effects of fallout on animals. In 1957 in the Priscilla test 700 anesthe-tized pigs were put in stations at various distances from ground zero to simulate the impacts on humans.

A large number of tests were conducted in 1958 in anticipation of a proposed test ban treaty between the U.S. and Soviet Union, but after it failed to be enacted the U.S. resumed mostly underground testing at the Nevada Test Site and atmospheric testing in the Pacific. Eventually, on August 5, 1963, the U.S. and Soviet Union signed the Limited Test Ban Treaty, banning tests in the atmosphere, as well as in the ocean and in space.

FELIX DE PAULA—*Trinity*

Felix De Paula

There were 45 engineers and about as many MP's at the Trinity site. It was kind of hard because we were restricted to the camp. Some of these men had just spent two or three years over in the South Pacific. They were shipped up to Los Alamos and thought they had done their time but they were stuck with the rest of us for God knows how long. More and more people from Los Alamos started to come down. They were setting up experiments. The population grew to almost 450. These Los Alamos people were in the know. They came on Monday and left on Friday. They were the commuters and it was hard for the rest of us to swallow.

The craftsmen didn't know why they were building miles of telephone poles. You'd sink a post in the ground and bolt a few arms across the top for stringing the wires. The job I wound up doing gave me a lot of freedom. I was the sanitation man of the camp. We had to go into town every day to haul 5,000 gallons of water, our only source of potable water for the camp. It gave me a little taste of freedom.

Nobody wanted my job, garbage man, but I remembered the Depression when we had to take whatever we could. My dad had a friend who was a garbage man. When he left the house each day he wore a white shirt, a jacket, and carried a small briefcase. When he got to the job he changed into his uniform. When the depression hit, who had jobs: teachers, g-men, and police. Now he had a steady paycheck and eventually managed to buy his own home.

The MP's had their horses and on Sunday they'd have polo games. They used broomsticks as their battering rams. Then they brought a pool table into our little PX and later set up a movie screen because our lieutenant realized we needed some kind of entertainment. In contrast, General Groves was much harder on us. He came down and couldn't understand why we were lying around on a Sunday. He wanted us working seven days a week. The lieutenant went along with a wink and a nod and told us to fake it on Sundays. We were still able to take out the jeeps and chase antelope all over the desert.

First of all, they simulated a test of the equipment. They detonated 100,000 pounds of dynamite. They built a massive platform and filled it up with countless boxes of explosives. They then blew it up and that was to calibrate their instruments. I managed somehow to sleep through that. Then when they were ready to detonate the bomb we were told to come out of the barracks in full field dress. They gave us dark glasses and we were placed behind an earthen mound and told to face away from the blast.

I was approximately 15 miles from Ground Zero. After it blew we turned to face it with those dark glasses on. It had rained that night and the weather was kind of miserable. They detonated around 5:00 A.M. To show you how naïve I was, it didn't mean too much to me—a tremendous cloud and so far away. But the older men, one in particular, Pop Borden, had a totally different reaction. Pop Borden had worked with a lot of dynamite back in New York state. He used to blow up stumps and had a better fix on what had just occurred. For a few days he was speechless and when he did speak he said it was the most devastating thing he had ever seen in his life. But for me at 19, it hardly registered. It was only after they dropped the bombs on Japan that I realized, my God, this is what had been going on in those long, hot months in Alamogordo.

ROBERT CAMPBELL—*Director of Testing in Both Locations*

Robert Campbell

For the Greenhouse test in 1951, Edward Teller wondered what went on inside the fireball. All we had been doing was photographing the outside. We put a group together, mainly engineers, and made a vessel, a cylinder with valves on both ends. We put it out there [beneath the bomb], and let it be engulfed. Close the valve and see what was in there. It was a radio chemistry type thing. The cylinder was 8-10 inches in diameter, an inch and a half thick, and a meter long. To make them close we made projectiles that were driven by black powder. We took them to the islands and placed them 50 feet from the bottom of a 300 ft. tower that had 10 kilotons of explosives on it. They were engulfed in the fireball. We recovered them with a C-2 wrecker, … 6 vehicle with a crane attached. We wore a standard anti-contamination suit. There was no shielding in it but it kept the dirt off. We took them apart and their insides were clean, no results.

In the summer of 1951, the same guy who got into radioactive sampling suggested another change. There was a job that had to be done. It wasn't like building a bomb. To test things atmospherically you need a recording station, bunkers, shields, collimators, and factories to produce liquid nitrogen. You need all sorts of crap built. To get that you go to the experimenters and find out what the hell he needs. Then you describe that to an architect engineer who designs something and produces drawings. Then you check to make sure that's what is needed and you build it.

There are all sorts of things you want to know about a bomb when it goes off. The main thing is to determine how many neutrons are released. A partial answer came from measuring the rate at which they are produced. If you take E to the alpha T, where E is the constant and T is time, the alpha is a variable. You measure that and you get a generation rate of neutrons. That was done by having a detector, which looked like a big vacuum tube on the end of a coaxial cable [a cable with a central core and a series of external windings around it for added strength]. At the time of Greenhouse, the coaxial was rigid copper, three and a half inches in diameter. It had a three-fourths center conductor that ran from the bombsite all the way to the recording station.

But this wouldn't fly for Mike [another bomb test], which was much too powerful and would destroy the cable before the information could be transmitted. Could we use a vacuum to speed up the transmission? A vacuum wasn't feasible but we could build a box-like tunnel and fill it with helium. And that's precisely what we did; a box 12 feet square and 4,000 feet long. We used polyethylene bags inside to prevent leakage. We flew in plane-loads of plywood and pressed everybody on the island who could hammer a nail into service. The tunnel was built in record time.

There were nine shields, collimators with holes in them that extended down the tunnel. They had to be precisely aligned. You had a detector on one end, a converter really. The collimators, once properly aligned, allowed the light signal to pass unobstructed to its destination. That was a real surveying problem because it was long enough to have to consider the curvature of the earth. The engineers who constructed it didn't trust just anybody to calculate it. They figured it out in the home office in Los Angeles and sent instructions as to how to align the shields.

Well, we got the damned thing built. You take a source and send it down to the cab end of the tunnel and look at it with the detector in the recording station. No dice! We can't see it. There were powers of ten all over the blackboard that evening [engineers and scientists trying to figure out the problem mathematically]. Finally, a surveyor came in real sheepishly and said he knew how to fix it. That was Marty Curan, who was in charge of the crew that set the shields. The shields were adjustable and somehow they managed to misread the instructions. They did a quick correction and by the next day everything was working like a charm. That plywood tunnel, it worked. It was quick and dirty but it did the job.

The biggest thing I had witnessed prior to the hydrogen bomb was a 50-kiloton explosion. This one was 11 or 12 megatons. Yeah, it was larger, pretty exciting. But that's the next thing that I got involved with, the translation from the physicist to the engineer, to construction, and back and forth, coordinating among all these people. There were a lot of nuts and bolts and details to take care of. I did this until 1957. The engineering part got pretty routine. I was apprenticed to the job of Test Director. Somebody in this testing game had to be in charge. I was trained by Bill Ogle [the Test Director].

We worked not only at Eniwetok, but the same group worked at the Nevada Test Site on an alternating year schedule. It was ongoing, the testing. I ended up doing it for 25 years. We started testing in 1957 in Nevada and I retired in 1982. NTS was closed in 1992. There was a two-year moratorium in 1958 during which time I headed up the Rover Project [an elaborate project that designed and built reactors in Los Alamos and tested in Nevada and gave many people work during the testing ban]. All we were ever doing was supporting the people who were getting their data. They were the show [the scientists who got all the attention]. The scientists deserve a lot of credit for their work but there is another group of people, a large group whose contribution is often overlooked. They are the support staff and they are goddamned important. Sometimes the scientists barely recognize the army of critical support they are receiving. They take it for granted, a big mistake.

PAUL GUTHALS—*Air Sampling in the Mushroom Cloud*

I was Project Leader for bomb cloud sampling. Our sampling people were Air Force people and we flew with them in their planes. With my Air Force background I had the job of making a "fit" between the civilian scientists and their way of doing things and the military methodology. We had to make the calculations as to what kind of activity we had to do in order to bring home the samples that others wanted and needed. Those samples were used to determine what the fission yield of the devices was.

One of my primary responsibilities was keeping these pilots safe. We used integrating dosimeters, rate meters, and so on. I was in direct communication with the pilots in flight. I also supervised the recovery operations when we got back to base. The mushroom cloud loses its identity in 15 to 30 minutes because of the heavy winds. At altitude they are much stronger than they are on the ground. Typically, we only made our penetrations after the cloud stabilized, after it quit rising.

The airplane we used was the B-57. These were two-engine jets. They were the "grandchildren" of the British airplane. It was a tandem, two-person cockpit, which enabled both the front and backseat to have an unobstructed view. The capability of the airplane for altitude was close to 55,000 feet. We recovered the samples from the airplanes mechanically, remotely reaching into the compartments and placing the filters into a lead "pig" and bringing them back to the Lab for analysis. There the chemistry was done on them and we made critical measurements that we were interested in.

We did a lot of testing in Eniwetok and Bikini, and later at the Nevada Test Site. We did a very high altitude test on Johnson Atoll, which is southwest of the Hawaiian Islands, and not so far as the others. We did our last big overseas operation over Christmas Island. We borrowed it from the British. This operation was principally airdrops from B-52's. By this I mean air detonations. A lot of the Nevada tests were surface detonations, or they were attached to high towers or balloons. I may have been fortunate or unfortunate, depending on how you look at it, but I was the person who was airborne on more detonations than anyone else in the world.

There was a very significant effort to know where the debris was going to come down. Very significant. Before you did a test there were all kinds of briefings. Typically we had a general officer who chaired the evaluation board. One of the major factors in making the decision was the weather, the predictions of downwind deposition. Keep in mind that some of these detonations went above 50,000 feet, so you went through "sheer" levels, where one might be going this way and the next, the other way. It made it difficult for the meteorologists to get their hands around it.

You may recall that there were some South Sea Islanders who got some fallout that wasn't predicted. There were also some Japanese fishermen who weren't where they [the military] thought they should be and got some too.

In these shots there was not a vaporization and re-condensation, there were pieces of material blown apart. They were much bigger, obviously, and they came down quicker than the material that was vaporized and re-condensed (so that the particles are minute and fall much more slowly). This is the reason they are carried such a long way. The country did investigations and monitoring a long, long way from the origin site. There were actually worldwide monitoring networks on the ground that read fallout months later.

MIKE PADILLA—*Island Decontamination Cloud Sampling*

Mike Padilla

I went to the Tech School at the Amarillo Air Force base and studied jet engine mechanics. At Kirtland I was assigned to the 4925th Test Squadron Sampling under the 4925th Test Group. This was in 1953. I was trained to support the pilots of the F-84's whose business it was to fly into the mushroom cloud and bring out samples of the radioactive particles. I was crew chief. I took care of the aircraft and made sure it was always in top operating condition. We were training for a long, top-secret mission whose destination was unknown. We found out later we were destined for the South Pacific and an island they called Eniwetok.

It was quite an experience there. We did a lot of practicing with aircraft going up every day. The B-36, the mother plane, was there too. It was filled with engineers and scientists overseeing the complex operation. When it came time for the real thing, all our tents were rolled up. This was 3:30 A.M. All aircraft that were not going to be flying were lashed down. We had two little hangers for maintenance and their doors were left open while every bit of equipment inside was secured. We were dressed in our protective overalls when the big plane started its engines. It took off and planned to stay airborne throughout the long day ahead. Our planes didn't move until after detonation.

Everything was in place when they came on the loudspeaker. That's when they marched us over to the runway and got us in position. Get in the prone position, away from the blast, cover your face. We had masks and goggles. What really got me was when they detonated that nuclear device. It was a hydrogen bomb. Everything lit up and it was 78 miles away. My eyes were as closed as I could make them but the light penetrated like an x-ray. It went dead quiet and then the loudspeaker told us that in a minute you will feel the first shock wave, with another to follow. There'll be a large boom and the island may shake. Oh man, the light and then the island did shake. We were flat on the runway. A second shock wave followed, then tremors. Now the loudspeaker said, remove your mask and turn around and face the blast. I got up and turned and my God, it was like I was right there. The mushroom was coming up. First you could only see the top, and then the bottom came into view—60,000-100,000 feet high.

Then it was time for us to do our work. We sent three planes up at a time. We got into position to receive them after they had made their pass into the cloud. They put me on a forklift with a crate on it and as soon as the pilot landed we opened the canopy. I helped the pilot out. He was in protective clothing too. As soon as we got him out, the other two guys locked all the explosives charges for the ejection seat. The monitors were right with us checking for radiation levels. We were told to strip off our clothing, both pilot and crew, and head for the emergency showers that were nearby. We would scrub and scrub and then get checked again. I took 12 showers in a matter of 90 minutes one day. We were running multiple aircrafts, recovering the filters, putting them in the lead pigs, [thick-walled boxes made of lead] and sending them off to Los Alamos. We couldn't spend more than three or four minutes doing this retrieval work so we worked in rotation.

The decontamination process took a week. We washed the planes daily with high- pressured hoses. Our pumps went right into the ocean—salt water first, fresh water second. Sometimes we used GUNK, a chemical agent in areas where the radiation liked to hide.

After a week I got lucky. They told me I could get into a plane and see what we accomplished there. There was no Bikini Atoll, just a deep, blue hole in the ocean. We flew at 15,000 feet. You could see the ships that were placed so many miles away from Ground Zero. The ones within forty miles were flipped over with hulls in the air. But what amazed me was that the island disappeared, leaving only a gaping wound in the ocean.

JACK AEBY—*Photography/Health Physics*

TRINITY:

I was not one of the professional photographers at Trinity. I merely brought along my 35 millimeter camera, hoping that I might be able to get a decent shot of the blast. The place was crawling with "serious" photographers with big cameras, all the bells and whistles. When it came time for the shot I grabbed a folding chair and steadied the camera on the back of it. The result was the only color photograph of the detonation that was produced for history on that day. It was used by the theoretical team to make the early measurements of the yield: they could measure where I was, the focal length, diameter of the fireball, and what fraction of a second after the blast that it was shot.

BIKINI:

After that I went to work for Brixner, the senior Lab photographer, filming at Bikini for three months. The operation was supposed to be three shots—an underwater, a surface shot, and an air drop. The first was the air drop, so they organized a fleet made up of captured German and Japanese vessels. The target vessel was the Yokohama. In the meantime we shot off flash bombs [intense flash bulbs] and adjusted our camera bases. We had three large towers erected on Bikini at sweeping angles focused on the drop zone.

We shot off the Scania [type of camera] and the fast-X, 35mm. That shot 3,000 exposures a minute. We were doing diagnostic photography; we wanted to know the yield from this. We also used some Air Force aerial cameras that were quite large. We would have to pull a wide sheet of film through the camera at a rapid rate. By doing this we sped the camera up. Normally they would go "whoosh, click, whoosh, click" for aerial photography. We disengaged the shutter and dragged a 100 feet of film as fast as we could pull. We just hoped that it hit the moment of explosion. This method did not produce a typical image, but just a "V" of light, an exposure. When you first start the fission reaction, it goes up to a high peak, then drops off to zero, then goes off in a regular pattern. Anyway, we wanted to know the estimate of yield when that occurred.

We went back in as soon as the lagoon was cleared. The first shot, the one that the Air Force dropped, missed the target by 1,500 yards. Our cameras were pointed off in another direction so we didn't get much, except what the wide-angle lens salvaged. They pulled us out, away from the lagoon. Then afterwards they cleared the lagoon and declared it "radioactive free." The boats could come back in and start the operation. The fleet area was essentially off limits. That's not where the research boats parked, at the target area, but somewhere down island [away from Ground Zero]. We got in, got our film out, and re-loaded for the next test that we expected in days. There were 30 participants from Los Alamos, called the Joint Task Force 7; the overall number was in the thousands.

I left the Lab for several years and re-trained in health physics. Our duty at the test sites involved going in with recovery groups after the shots to set up monitoring conditions. We adhered to rules and regulations having to do with people wearing film badges, etc. We manned checkpoints to make sure that the right people went to the right place. It was a matter of personal monitoring to make sure that a person stayed within the prescribed limits. We started out in the early years with a 15R annual limit, later it was dropped to 5R, and now I think we're down to 3R.

CLEAN-UP:

In the 1970s on Eniwetok we worked hard to clean up the island. First we laid out grid in each area and took soil samples, both surface and deeper. We had a portable Lab set up to analyze these samples. This was a three-year process. So what did we do with all that contaminated soil? Do you remember the large blast on Elugelab that disappeared an island? The Bravo experiment just did in that island. It created a vast hole in the ocean floor. So they set up an operation to take all the contaminated material, mix it with concrete in a slurry, and pump it down into the hole. They hauled in barges of concrete every week for three years. It was an impressive operation, but I still wouldn't eat a banana off Picnic Island! Once they got the hole filled up to island level they poured a thick concrete cap on it— filled, done, finito.

NEVADA TEST SITE:

Our group ran the weather section and had the say so over go or no go, depending on the weather predictions. Our director, Norris Bradbury, made it very clear that no Lab activity is worth putting people in harm's way. But, believe me, the pressure to do these tests was very great. We were well aware of the risks and took every precaution to limit the risks, but things did go wrong occasionally. A wind could switch direction at the last moment and blow over St. George, for instance. And rather than warn people and cause panic, we sent in teams to monitor the effects. We knew what the fallout was, where it was, and had a reasonable grasp of the curve risk. You couldn't very well deal with long term problems like strontium-90. What was that going to do to the cattle industry? Was it going to contaminate milk next year? You couldn't measure that. When the fallout cloud passes, it's gone.

JAY HAMMEL—*Low Temperature Physicist*

[The following passage is from an interview conducted by Leslie Hammel Turk, Jay's daughter, and is essentially an appeal to the Laboratory, written in his last months of life, to accept responsibility for his fatal illness.]

On September 19, 1989, my thyroid was surgically removed and was found to contain an extremely rare and aggressive malignant tumor. Examination of the tissue found radiation damage in the non-tumorous lobe of the thyroid. The result of the biopsy, along with my history of radiation exposure in the Redwing Series of Pacific tests in 1956, resulted in the general agreement among LANL experts and my physician that the cancer was the result of this exposure.

The operation in which I was exposed was run with the objective of shooting as many tests as possible during the series. This policy bypassed, to a large extent, the personal safety of some of the people directly involved with the device being tested. I was particularly vulnerable to this way of operating because I was completely unfamiliar with the operation: it was my first involvement in a test, and I arrived late in the test series. I wasn't briefed as to the safety issues, such as the areas that would be radiation hazards or what experience the health division had with background radiation at the test site where I would be required to work. Safety was being ignored even at the basic level of warnings that radiation was present in certain areas, informing people that fallout was expected, or in one case, that a high level of fallout was actually taking place.

There were three places where I was exposed to high levels of bomb debris [a large amount of radio-iodine]: first, crossing Ground Zero one day after the shot; second, being caught outside on Eniwetok during a rainstorm containing heavy fallout from a large shot on Bikini; and third, spending a large amount of time on the Huron shot barge where we prepped for the shot while the barge was in a highly contaminated moorage in the lagoon.

I was responsible for the preparation and monitoring of new components for two devices being tested. These shots were to take place during the latter half of the Redwing series. The series managers were so anxious to get these shots fired that they arranged a special MATS [high priority military] flight from Honolulu for me two days before my scheduled departure from Eniwetok. I arrived on Perry Island late at night, and early the next morning I was flown by helicopter to the site of my first shot. The shot tower was pointed out to me, and I walked to that point to meet the LANL technicians who were getting things ready. I needed to get acquainted with how the device was going to be placed and how the components that I was responsible for were situated. Upon arrival I was told by people at the tower that I had just walked across Ground Zero of the test on the previous day. There were no warnings or barriers, nothing. I was completely new to the test site, got no briefing, and was sent off in a helicopter with no monitor.

The Huron shot was on a barge in Bikini Lagoon. The scientific people spent all day, every day for two weeks preparing for the shot. Nights were spent in camp on Bikini. During this time a tritium "sniffer" was used to monitor for any possible tritium leaks. The sniffer was a proportional counter developed at the University of California to sample air for the presence of tritium. While we were working on the barge the sniffer always had a high background signal caused by the contaminated atmosphere of the lagoon. The signal was not able to identify the radioactive source or give a quantitative value on the amount of radiation. I told Roy Reider [Health Division Group Leader] of my concern and he said not to worry and get on with the preparations because HD was on top of the problem. We finished our discussion and he jokingly added," It's good for you."

I know a tritium level at our Lab would not have been tolerated. After spending a lot of time on the "hot" barge getting the device ready, the final day arrived with all the Bikini personnel except Gaden Felt, the Air Force Colonel, a tech [Ben Maestas], and me on a ship 30 miles away. I had the very undesirable duty of aborting the shot 30 seconds before shot time because of a drop in one of our monitor signals. Bob Burton and I had to go back on the barge in foul weather to disarm the device and find out about the sensitive components of the device. After an analysis of the data from the device, it was determined that the abort was required because of the failure of the CMRD component. This event delayed the tests and caused me further exposure to shot debris.

Several weeks were required to reinstall the replacement sent out from Los Alamos. Just prior to the second Huron shot I was on Eniwetok when a very high yield Livermore device was shot on Bikini. As far as I know, there was no general alarm given that a large amount of fallout was expected on Eniwetok and that people should take shelter. During the storm I received a film badge of 6R [6 Rem, which is well over the legal limit of 4] while others received considerably more.

I am now suffering from the presence of a very aggressive

thyroid cancer as a result of my experiences in the Redwing test of 1956.

RALPH PARTRIDGE—*Electrical Engineer/Physicist*

Ralph Partridge

I was trained in electrical engineering and physics, electro-magnetic field theory. My work always involved nuclear weapons testing. It was a tremendous source of gamma rays, neutrons, and x-rays, with which we could do science as well as advanced engineering. I was designing advanced instrumentation for making measurements on nuclear devices. From 1955-1965 I was measuring the radio wave pulses that are put out when a bomb goes off—an electro-magnetic pulse.

So we did underground testing and it got more and more elaborate in order to yield more and more data. We learned how to extract underground data under very difficult circumstances. You dig a hole one-quarter of a mile deep. You take a bomb and place it on a 100-foot rack [a cylindrical steel column that acts as a cradle to hold the bomb and all its connecting cables], an elevator type of thing, and drop it into the bottom of that hole. Then you try and get the data that you'd be hard pressed to get in a laboratory environment. You know the digital cameras that are so popular now? We essentially invented them. They had to go down the hole and snap a picture, not in visible light, but with high energy x-rays. The bomb puts out its own x-rays, so it makes an image of itself. Those impinge on the fluorescent screen, a piece of plastic that lights up invisible light with the image of the pattern of x-rays that hit it, and then our camera snaps a picture of that. We had to get our image in a tremendous hurry before the camera was vaporized. We went through a lot of cameras! You get the exposure that lasts for only a millionth of a second and transmit it to the surface before the camera is destroyed.

When the shot goes off underground it is extremely hot. You've got this gaseous liquid and solid stuff down there and the ground is porous. The melted rock starts to cool and the surface hardens. The ceiling will eventually fall back in. The dirt above collapses and a chimney forms above it all the way to the surface. Then the surface of the ground falls back and all this compaction minimizes the chance of any gas escaping. We hardly ever had any radiation leakage to speak of.

After the shot, KABOOM, it would take anywhere from a few seconds to several hours for the crater to form. Immediately afterward the radiation monitors were the first ones allowed in after the helicopter flyovers. They would check for radiation and then we would head in and walk right into the crater to salvage our very valuable fiber optic cables. We'd go right down to where the cable emerged from the ground and cut it off. We had no problem with radiation; it just wasn't there.

How many tests was I involved with over the years? That's a tough one. We fired close to 1,000, so I must have been involved with at least half of them. In the atmospheric test we might be only six miles away. They were bigger in the Pacific, so we'd typically be out 20 miles. Being that close, we probably got more radiation than most people. The people who received more than we did were the pilots who actually penetrated the cloud after the detonation. Also, the military that we put in much closer than our positions probably got more radiation. We got some pretty good doses, well above the legal limits of 4R.

There was one shot when we got lost in the desert. We stopped and got out of the car to find out where we were and it turned out that we were standing at the base of the tower where the bomb had been detonated! We were actually standing on the concrete slab that was dished from the blast, and we got so much exposure that our badges just turned black and nobody could read them. We were off the dial because we got lost out there.

It's a funny phenomenon: you have a desert full of sagebrush and a few roads here and there, or really not quite roads but bulldozed paths where you could drive. When the bomb goes off, KABLOOIE, it loosens all the surface dirt and big rocks pop up and when you return the land is strewn with boulders. Where's the road? You get lost.

My first shot on the islands was the Mike Shot, the first thermo-nuclear bomb in 1952. It went larger than expected. It was different from a fission bomb and they didn't know how to predict it very well. When we went in on recovery we traveled on a DUKW, an amphibious boat/car. Every day in order to get to work we had to go past the bomb as it was being constructed; it was like building a large building, constructing that bomb. It wasn't droppable. After the shot we flew over and observed that the entire island was gone. When it came time, the radiation people began flying over to check levels. They decided that it was down enough to allow us in. We could take our boat around the giant crater to our work station. We could only stay for 20 minutes max, then get the hell out.

We got into the concrete bunker and there was no radiation inside. We had to haul the sandbags away from the door and pry open the steel doors. Once inside we were faced with a lot of electrical wiring that had to be disconnected. We were in a big hurry so we started ripping out wires, helter-skelter. We forgot about the 12-volt battery. I made a cross circuit and some of the wires started to burn red hot. The insulation vaporized and produced a terrible chemical smell. We were sure it was dangerous but couldn't go outside because of the radiation. We couldn't stay inside either because of the chemicals, so we ducked outside for a quick breath of air, then back inside to rip wires and get the film out of the cameras. Back and forth we went while frantically waving for a rescue from the boat.

This was the best time of my life, doing things under those kinds of conditions; it was almost like combat. It's an interesting thing, in my personal philosophy. I wasn't in WW II, or Korea, or Vietnam, but I felt like I had to do something for my country. If I went out and did a job that involved a certain amount of personal danger, it made me feel better inside, that you were sharing something with the men who were out there getting shot at.

CASEY STEVENS—*Technician*

Casey Stevens

I was in J-10, which was a part of J Division, the diagnostic and testing division. We did all the testing in Nevada. I used to commute every week for six months at a time. They used to call us the longest commuters in the world. We'd leave here [New Mexico] on Sunday, stay at NTS [Nevada Test Site] all week, or two or three weeks at a clip, then return on Friday night, come home, change clothes, and fly out again on Sunday.

I worked the tunnels and the vertical shafts, putting in the in-strumentation down the hole. The first thing they did was to dig a hole, 3,600 to 4,000 feet deep. They dug it with a special rig designed by the engineers at the test site. They could drill a hole anywhere from two to eight feet in diameter or larger. Normally they drilled two sets of holes next to each other, a personnel hole and another for the equipment. The equipment hole was the one that took the rack. The personnel hole was approximately five feet in diameter where the elevator was installed. Just like in the mines. They used the same signals and the dead man's stick in the case of trouble. That system will automatically lock and stop the elevator. I got stuck in there one of those times.

On the bottom you had horizontal tunnels where the experi-ment was set up. I put in eight, ten, twelve hours at a time in the holes and side tunnels or "drifts." The rock formation was sand-stone, very soft material that you could scrape. Some areas of the tunnels had to be reinforced to guard against cave-ins. If you worked in the holes you could be there for a period of months getting equipment and cable ready before the rack was lowered that actually held the device.

You are putting in data-collecting electronic equipment down there. It was optical instrumentation that would transmit infor-mation through cables or tubes to the surface. That's when the rack went down and they had all the rest of the instrumentation in it that was needed. Then the hole was backfilled and covered. The cables, of course, came out of the ground and went to the diagnostic trailer where the information gathering instruments were located. Essentially that was it—you could be on a project for two or three months, depending on how complicated the bot-tom was. A lot of work went into those shots. One of them could cost upwards of 10 million dollars.

As I mentioned before, I was trapped in one of them. See, each time you go down, if there was no one down there, you have to have a miner with you. They employed miners at the site. That was the rule. This particular time there was nobody else in the tunnel. I was the first one to go down. I went with this fellow who was attached to me. Every time I went down he seemed to be the guy on top who was ready to join me. Poor guy got killed eventually. He got cut right in half by one of the elevators.

He did a lot of crazy things that I cautioned him about. I told him to watch out and not take those kinds of risks. There were these side drifts and he wanted to get into them for some reason, so he would jump off the elevator and didn't quite make it one time. He fell back against the elevator and that was the end of it.

Doing that kind of work you had to be precise. If you weren't, the routine wouldn't go as planned. One screw up and you could blow a multi-million dollar test. There were optical components, oscilloscopes, and often we blew them up in the shot. Another time the whole station was wiped out because the instruments became radioactive. The tubes that contained the cables had charges set around them. As soon as the shot went off those charges crimped the pipes and all radiation was choked off before it made it to the surface. For some reason the pipes failed to get crimped one time—like that shot years and years back where they contaminated southwest Utah, the pinch method just didn't work.

ANTHONY MONTOYA— *Radiological Control Technician*

Anthony Montoya

The first test in Nevada was called Ranger and they asked me to go as a health monitor. They didn't have any at the time, military or otherwise. So I was in Nevada for Buster-Jangle, Ranger, and many more. In the tests, all these guys have experiments going on at different distances from Ground Zero. Naturally, the tests [the individual experiments that the scientists were conducting around the detonation] were being exposed to radiation, or the neutron burst of the bomb. After the detonation, at a certain time afterwards the teams would go in and recover the samples. They wanted to get them ASAP so as not to lose any data. I would go in and make a judgment as to whether it was getting too hot to stay. We took readings and figured the time as to how long we could be there without getting overexposed.

I was in charge. You had to have small groups go in to be able to control them. Normally we had dry runs; we'd go in and they knew exactly what they would do. They would time themselves to recover the samples. There were times when you had to overexpose some people. It was essential, but then you would have to take him out and he would be through. At that time the maximum exposure was 5R per annum.

I was assigned to the radiochemistry people. The group leader, Charlie Brown, asked for me all the time. He's dead now, as is most of his group. They were the people who determined how high the explosion went, how many kilotons it yielded according to their calculations.

I always figured I had my instruments to guide me. That was my sense of security. I would double check them to make sure they were working properly. It was the poor people who didn't have the instruments who got overexposed. They might go into an area by accident and not know what they were getting into. In areas where you know what to expect, you protect yourself and you are not going to get exposed. If by some chance you do get exposed, you get the hell out of there fast.

The first alpha monitor was called the "pee-wee." I worked with Howard Eberline when he first developed it. It was huge and really heavy. We carried it with straps around our necks and lugged it all over the place. I was young and I had a family to support. You needed the job. You figured that these guys were smart enough to figure out what is safe and what is not. I didn't know enough about it to doubt them. I took classes and learned about the different types of radiation, what was emitted, what the half-lives were.

One time during Operation Plumb Bob they had a balloon test. They needed a reading at Ground Zero really badly. It was a few days after the blast and I figured I could get in and out without getting "burned out." By that I mean getting my full exposure and then being through. I went in and later saw my exposure on my medical record; I got 2R.

Since I was involved with the group and the testing, the scientists were familiar with me. They requested that I come to TA-49 and head up health physics. We worked day and night. The site was located out near Bandelier. There was nothing there until we started drilling. The holes were not nearly as deep as at Nevada, only 100 feet deep. The tests were overseen by Bob Campbell, the director. They would do dry runs, locking down the area so no one could stray into the restricted area. They had to watch the winds very carefully and make sure they were not blowing toward Los Alamos. Radiochemistry used Godiva to ignite the explosive test. Godiva was the reactor that sent a neutron down. They sent the neutron flux down and ignited the weapon. The hole was backfilled and the only thing that was open was the chute that would come out sideways for the sample box. The samples came up into a steel box that was sealed. So they would run up to the box, get the sample out, and get out of there as quickly as possible. They had a Lab up there so they could do the analysis right away.

I was the first man in to take the readings and make sure that nobody would get hurt. I took two instruments all the time, didn't trust just one. The only thing that was active was Godiva. She was sitting right on top of the test. You didn't hear the explosion or anything like that. None of it went critical. You found out how close you could get without exceeding the limit. They found out what they wanted to find out, but I'm not quite sure what. I could tell by their expressions, they would say "O.K., that's it," and then they went on to Nevada.

ACCIDENT:

It was an incident really. We were monitoring somebody in a virgin hole and quite by accident found that he had a shoe that was contaminated. It shouldn't have been hot. So we started checking the area and found a reading in the virgin hole. It wasn't a big reading but we were obliged to check the workers, many of whom were from Chimayó. It was Christmas and we ate biscochitos as we went from house to house, as everyone was preparing for the holidays. We worked on Christmas Eve and Christmas Day. We never found any homes that were hot, but we found clothing and shoes. It wasn't a big deal.

They wanted me to monitor the hole. So I got dressed up in the appropriate gear and a crane slowly lowered me down. I monitored the walls, little by little. It was in the crevices that I found the high readings. It was alpha that I was reading. The only way alpha could hurt you was by inhalation or if you had an open wound of some kind. So I went in there and found the alpha and none of it had gone critical.

ON SCIENTISTS:

If you were working with scientists, they didn't pay any attention to you. You tell them that they can't do something, or that they have to clean up their mess, and they just look at you. They're God. Now it may be more under control, but during my time they ruled. They were getting that bomb and they didn't want to hear anything from anybody. Sometimes we'd have to clean up after them ourselves.

LOS ALAMOS REVISITED

Chapter Four

HEALTH AND SAFETY

When I ended each one of my 150 interviews I asked the same question: "If you had to do it over again, would you have followed the same path that led you to Los Alamos?" The responses were split down the middle. The first group answered in the affirmative. "The Lab provided secure jobs for myself and my family and I have encouraged my children to follow in my footsteps." The other half of the group was adamant that they never would have gone to Los Alamos if they had known the risks. Their health was too high a price to pay for job security. They would under no circumstances encourage their children to work there. Not surprisingly, illness and death were the factors that caused such different views. For those who were fortunate enough to come through 40 or more years of employment without serious consequences there were positive rewards, but for those whose names grace our memorial list, a number in the hundreds, the price was much too high. As our conversations unfolded, I was often told that this particular worker was the last of his crew alive. Ruben Montoya, who spent 20 years in Sigma Building, kept lists of the men who died and there were 48 names from that one building alone. These men, primarily in their 40s and 50s, died of a variety of cancers. There was also a pattern of men who managed to get through to retirement and then died within the following year. This is a hidden legacy of the Los Alamos years. The Lab claimed it had little knowledge of the hazards, but safety precautions were very lax. What the Lab did and did not know is certainly open to examination. Gene Westerhold told me about the use of asbestos to insulate pipes: "We came out looking like snowmen, covered in the dust, then blew ourselves off and sat down to our lunch." Gene was convinced that the Lab knew it was carcinogenic 20 years before they made it public. Ray Casias was in a class discussing the use of respirators through the years. The oldest one on the table was one he was old enough to have actually used and the filter was made of asbestos! Phil Schofield simply states he heard his superiors say "the workers were expendable."

Joe Martinez, a forty-year maintenance worker, mused about the fact that the current workers have things so much better. If his son found himself in a situation that he thought was dangerous he could file a complaint and get reassigned to another area. But when Martinez worked at the Lab, if you spoke a word of complaint about a hazardous job you were gone. So you kept your head down, mouth shut, and took your chances. Ben Ortiz was exposed to a variety of toxic chemicals in his work as a welder on the linear accelerator. Their safety meetings consisted of suggestions like keeping extension cords coiled up so no one tripped. As his symptoms grew more acute he sought help and the Lab doctors were unresponsive. He was eventually sent to a psychiatrist because they felt that his complaints were imaginary and that he could be having a problem with alcohol. I'm sure that some of the medical people at the Lab were perfectly competent, but the prevailing wisdom among the workers was that if you hoped to get a fair shake you had to travel outside the purview of the Lab and go to Albuquerque or beyond. Even some of the scientists received poor treatment when it came to getting the Lab to acknowledge responsibility for wrongdoing. Jay Hammel was exposed to extreme levels of radiation in the fifties at Bikini and was convinced that his late developing thyroid cancer was caused by this exposure. In his last months of life he pleaded with the Laboratory to recognize this and warn other veterans who might be experiencing a similar fate. They turned him down.

The perception of health problems in the community of Los Alamos is very different depending on whom you talk to. I was struck by the differences when I spent an afternoon visiting two different families who lived only blocks away from one another in town. The first family was a Hispanic one that had come to Los Alamos in the 1940s and had remained in the same house all these years. After my interview was over with the man of the house, his wife joined us for coffee and the subject of cancer came up. She rattled off the names of eight or nine people in her immediate neighborhood who had all succumbed to cancer. It was really shocking. My next stop was to see a weapons special-ist, also a long-time resident. When I brought the topic up he immediately quoted some medical study that confirmed the fact that the rates of cancer in Los Alamos were within some kind of norm and there was no reason to be concerned. Such different views and such close neighbors.

Some workers took political action to address the health issues at LANL. The Los Alamos Project on Worker Safety (LAPOW) was organized by Ben Ortiz, who worked as a welder on the linear accelerator at the Clinton P. Anderson Meson Facility at Los Alamos, and Ken Silver, currently an associate professor of Environmental Health at East Tennessee State University. At the time, Silver was providing pro bono technical assistance to those workers and families trying to get compensation for their work-related illnesses. Ortiz and Silver, along with Huguette Sirgant, who lost her scientist husband to a rare cancer, began meeting with various Lab workers and union members, along with representatives from both Congressman Tom Udall and Senator Jeff Bingaman's offices in 1999 to discuss worker safety issues. A public meeting on March 18, 2000 was a historic day in Española, New Mexico. Over 700 people gathered at the Joseph Montoya Room at the Northern New Mexico Community

College to tell their stories of illness and loss due to their work at LANL. Senator Bingaman and Congressman Udall heard over 300 testimonials and promised to offer some relief. The rhetoric was sweet but the ensuing reality was anything but. What was remarkable to me was that so many were courageous enough to step forward and speak out, many for the first time. Some came on walkers, wheeling oxygen, supported by family members of several generations. Their strength and dignity was overpowering. Jerry Leyba, a worker's rights activist, expressed it this way: "You have the right as an employee to speak out. Don't be afraid, your voice counts. It is like the wolf that is coming after the sheep. If the sheep stands his ground, the wolf will back off. I say speak out but do it respectfully without anger or hate."

Jerry Leyba: the heart and soul of the LAPOWS. [this applies to both men]

Ben Ortiz

The LAPOW group began to organize by compiling a mailing list and sending out "action alerts." Leyba, who worked at the Lab initially as a radiological control technician and later for X-Division as a property administrator, contributed his experience as a member of CLER, Citizens for LANL Employee Rights, and UPTE, University Professional Technicians Employees (both of which are discussed in detail in the Whistleblower chapter). LAPOW continued to support the labor groups affiliated with the Lab and passed a resolution in support of the federal Energy Employees Occupational Illness Compensation Program Act (EEOICPA).

Congress enacted EEOICPA in 2001 to compensate nuclear workers who developed cancer and other serious diseases as a result of exposure to radiation and toxic substances in the workplace. EEOICPA created two programs through which claimants can seek compensation: Part B, which provides a one-time compensation package of $150,000 plus medical expenses for workers who have contracted one of twenty-two designated cancers because of job-related radiation exposure; and Part E, which provides up to $250,000 for lost wages and disabilities that resulted from job-related factors. The Department of Energy administered the EEOICPA claims program until November 2005 when, because of numerous instances of incompetence and corruption, Congress transferred administration to the Department of Labor. The DOL operates Resource Centers (RC) near nuclear weapons facilities throughout the country that are supposed to help claimants initiate their claims and guide them through the process. Those employees who worked at LANL from March 15, 1943 to December 31, 1975 and developed EEOICPA designated diseases (lung diseases and cancers) are being granted compensation under a Special Exposure Cohort (SEC) that became effective on July 22, 2007. SEC status means qualified workers do not have to go through a process that is supposed to "reconstruct the dose of radionuclides and other toxins to which they were exposed." Those workers who do not fall under the auspices of the SEC bear the burden of proving their claim. Many claimants, however, even with the assistance of Division of Energy Employee Occupational Compensation (DEEOIC) personnel, find it impossible to locate critical employment, exposure, and medical records necessary to substantiate their claims. In many cases it's been shown that these records no longer exist because they have been lost or destroyed by the agency or hospital responsible for them. This problem is further compounded when the claimant is the spouse or child of a deceased employee who doesn't have first-hand knowledge of the employee's history. Claimants have found that exposure records, which are critical to substantiating the amount and duration of exposure to radiation and other toxic substances, are often inaccurate and don't reflect the fact that claimants often worked at many different sites within the facility. Moreover, many claimants assert that they were periodically instructed by their supervisors to take off their dosimetry badges, which were the basis for monitoring their radiation exposure.

To try to rectify this situation, several bills were introduced into Congress to extend the SEC status. The Ray Ruiz Special Exposure Cohort Act, introduced in 2008 by then Congressman Tom Udall, extended the current SEC to include individuals who worked at LANL from 1976 to 1995, provided they are diagnosed with the cancers stipulated under the SEC and worked an aggregated total of 250 days at LANL. The bill is named for former State Representative Ray Ruiz, a LANL employee who developed cancer as a result of his work at the Lab and who died in 2004. Ruiz, his wife Harriet, and other tireless advocates were largely responsible for the establishment of the original SEC. The Charlie Wolf Act (named for a nuclear worker at Rocky Flats, who died of brain cancer), introduced by Colorado Senator Mark Udall in 2009 (cosponsored by Tom Udall) went even further by seeking "to expand the category of individuals eligible for compensation, improve the procedures for providing compensation, and improve transparency."

In 2008 LANL Security Guard Andrew Evaskovich submitted a petition on behalf of "service support employees who worked in areas at LANL with a history of radioactive material use from January 1, 1976 through December 31, 2005." Finally, in September of 2012, the Advisory Board on Radiation and Worker Health approved the petition and actually granted SEC status to *all* LANL workers who developed radiogenic cancers after having been employed for at least 250 days from January 1, 1976 to December 31, 1995. The Advisory Board continued to evaluate whether workers from 1995 through 2005 merited Special Exposure Cohort status, but in 2017 the National Institute for Occupational Safety and Health (NIOSH) denied the petition to extent the cohort status, claiming there is enough accurate data to conduct dose reconstruction on nuclear workers in that time period. It is more than likely that the Advisory Board will agree with the NIOSH assessment.

Nationally, at the time of the Special Exposure Cohort expansion, less than 28 percent of all claimants had been compensated: for every payment of $150,000 for radiation cancers under Part B, the government spent $45,000-50,000 on dose reconstructions alone (this figure includes multiple reconstructions for individual claimants because of appeals and new exposure data constantly coming to light). Obtaining SEC status is an overly cumbersome, time consuming, and expensive process fraught with bureaucratic demands and interference.

DARLEEN ORTIZ—*Daughter of Max Ortiz, Custodian*

My dad, Max Ortiz, started working in Los Alamos back in 1947-8. He was actually hired to work building the roads. He was then hired by the Zia Company, which was a janitorial service with the Lab at that time. He worked with them all the way through until he retired in 1975.

My dad was well known by a lot of people at the Lab, having worked there since its inception. He worked in many different sites. I can't recall all the locations. I wish he was alive to tell me. I do know that he worked in the machine shop, and he also did clean up. He cleaned the labs and offices of many scientists. He told me that the scientists used to tell him not to touch anything on the floor until they told him to. There was one scientist who used to crumble up paper and there were layers of it in every direction, but he couldn't touch it until he got the OK. I'm just a little leery now, because I know my Dad, if he swept up all that dust, he brought it home to us. My older sister, Linda Barela, is now suffering from a lung disease that is very strange to us. She's fifty now and came down with it about five years ago. She was two years old when we moved to Los Alamos. She went to school there and played all around, as all of us kids did. She told me a story that my dad had related that I was too small to remember myself. Dad used to like to take us kids to the dumpsites because there was a lot of copper wire we used to collect. He would sell it. We'd have to strip off the plastic casings. She said they were always looking through the dumpsites for wire. He knew where

These Quonset huts were brought into Los Alamos in 1943 as quick, easy housing: 750 square feet, divided down the middle with a sheet to provide a little privacy for the two families in each unit. They sprung up in the eastern community.

all the good stuff was.

Every day when my father came home we would run and jump all over him. Whatever he had on his clothes I'm sure we ended up getting all over us. He wasn't always clean when he came home, being a janitor and doing a lot of dirty work. It's horrible to say, but my dad didn't believe in showering more than once a week. He'd clean up in the morning but not shower. He grew up on a ranch in northern New Mexico outside of Las Vegas in Ribera and that was the way they did things. So every Friday night he would shower.

My sister and I have discussed that it could have been that we were contaminated by what came home with him on his coveralls, his work shirts, his shoes. He didn't change when he got home, either. His clothes were put with ours in the wash. We all did the laundry together.

My father used to do a lot of fishing. I learned how to hunt and fish from him. We used to go to a pond in Los Alamos. There was a little pier you could fish on. There was a ton of fish in there. We fished there a lot as well as the streams all around the town and the Rio [Grande], Santa Clara, all over. He was a hunter too. He hunted deer every year and would make jerky. My mom didn't like it fresh, it was too wild, but she'd eat it dry in fried potatoes and chile. My dad knew where, in the restricted sites, there was game. In the places they were told to hunt there weren't many deer. He knew where the deer were and he'd go find them. Who knows what the deer ate and what they drank. We ate the deer meat every year.

He would go on his lunch hour and pick piñon from the best places, again some of them in restricted areas. He'd bring home the biggest, fattest, piñon we'd ever seen. And every year we ate piñon. He was still picking the year before he died and I think I still had some in the freezer up until two years ago.

We used to eat so much that grew around there. I can't imagine that some of it wasn't contaminated. We used to eat monkey nuts. It was a tree that had these little tiny nuts that are kind of furry on the end but they have a little hard seed in them. Don't ask me how we knew to eat those things. You could eat all the meat off the outside and leave the seed. We ate a lot of those. Also flowers. You know how they put them in salads now? Well, we didn't have snacks. We were hungry a lot of the time and we would eat roses, carnations, and this orange and red flower that my mom used to grow that tasted like cloves. We ate acorns, the piñon, wild strawberries, and my mom would make us snow ice cream. She'd bring in some fresh snow and add a little milk and sugar and food coloring. We always drank water from the streams, of course. As a matter a fact, I did that all my life until I was a senior in high school. I drank from a stream in Hyde Park and I ended up with hepatitis. The water was so cool and clear, we never imagined it could hurt us. We also had a garden, a big one in the back. My dad grew tomatoes, radishes, carrots, everything.

My sisters used to play in all the canyons in Los Alamos. They told me that there was a playground where they'd climb down to get to it. They knew how to get up and down all those canyons. They did rock climbing and had little ladders to help. I was too young for all of that, but they remember being all over that place.

My oldest sister, Jo Ann, had breast cancer. My sister Linda has had several tumors removed from her toes. She says it's from her walking through the dumpsites. I was born with a tumor. It grew to the size of a jack ball and was on the back of my leg. They removed it when I was about two. It was traumatic for me. They brought me home from the hospital and I just wanted to play. I had stitches from the operation and when I went down the slide I tore the stitches wide open on a lip at the bottom of the slide. There was blood everywhere.

My mother had a miscarriage in her eighth month. I would have had a brother, two years younger. She then got a hysterectomy. He was full of tumors and she was full of tumors, too. There was nothing they could do for him. I watched a program the other night on T.V. that was pretty horrifying. It was about keeping body parts of the deceased for study. I sometimes wonder if our little baby brother wound up in a lab somewhere as a specimen … .

I only had the one tumor, but my mother said that at the time of my birth there was an emergency. Everyone was running in every direction. She could hear them out in the hall, despite her grogginess, saying, the Ortiz baby, the Ortiz baby. There was an alarm going off. She had no idea what was going on, but when she finally came to, she asked. They told her that I was born without a rectum opening and they had to create it. Come to think of it, that wouldn't have caused such an alarm.

My mother became very ill in 1990. She died in '91. My mother had always had health problems in Los Alamos. About a year before she was diagnosed with cancer, she had gone in to see her doctor and she was told she had polyps in her colon. They would try to remove one or two. They did that, and in the process found out that one of the polyps was cancerous. She was checked six months later, and everything seemed O.K. By Christmas she was beginning to get real tired and had chills. We took her in on Christmas Eve and that's when they diagnosed her as having cancer. They gave her two months to live and she died two months later. In 1990 my father noticed there was a small, discolored growth on his testicles. After my mother died he finally went to the doctor. She said to make sure he got it checked before she went into her coma. That summer, we all made him go to the doctor. It turned out to be cancer, skin cancer, a very rare form of it. It took many weeks before they could clearly diagnose the type. There was a lab in San Francisco that finally made the diagnosis.

They removed it and said, basically, he was fine. I guess he was OK after that. He was never one to complain. By Christmas in 1993 he had been feeling sluggish. We urged him again to see the doctor. It was the first week in January when they discovered his neck tumor. It wasn't noticeable at all from the outside. By the time they found it, he was told that it was too late. They couldn't remove it and it had already begun to spread. They tried to make him as comfortable as possible and gave him about four months to live. Sure enough, by the end of April he passed away. We took care of him at home. He refused any kind of life support. Same with my mother. We cared for her at home until she passed away, and we did the same for my father.

There was a doctor in Santa Fe, when my father was diagnosed, who was very interested in his history when we told him where he lived and worked. We were in a state of shock because we had just heard that he had cancer, so we were only half listening. We remember that he had a notebook and a bunch of questions. He would just go down the line, asking him all these questions about Los Alamos. My sister has his name and she was going to try and see the medical records to find out what his research was about.

At that time, we didn't have a clue. My awareness about all this came when I was invited to attend that first meeting [public meeting to discuss worker safety]. I was even reluctant to go at that time. I had no idea of the magnitude of the problem. If it can help anybody in the future or help anyone with possible diseases that are coming down the line, that's what I would like to do with our story. But, at the time, we weren't even thinking along these lines.

There have been a lot of unanswered questions in my family. Who really knows what we were exposed to and how much of this medical legacy is due to that exposure. We may never have the answers. Who knows what is in our systems and will continue to be through the generations? Radiation is still such a new science. I think they are now just beginning to find out things. I imagine the survivors of the bomb in Japan and their subsequent offspring may hold some of the answers for us.

They had little knowledge of all the health hazards in the early years. If they had any idea of the extent of the danger they would never have buried things as they did. Now a lot of the waste will be going to the WIPP site. Where did it go before?

Out the back door—out of sight, out of mind.

Knowing my father, because he was in the military and very loyal to his country, he probably would do it again. Just to be a part of history being made. He wasn't a brilliant scientist, he didn't have the background to play a major role, but was part of a team. He felt loyal to those scientists and even though he used to make fun of them, he did respect them. He'd do it again, even though they all used to talk to themselves. My Dad said they're all "locos"!

RUBEN MONTOYA—*Technician*

Ruben Montoya

I was working at Sigma Building in metallurgy. There were other metallurgists who came to work there. There was one guy, his name was Duncan, and he didn't like the way they were treating some of us. He quit because he couldn't put up with it. He said, "I'm sorry Ruben, about what they are doing to you." He was in charge of welding, the investigation of welding: they were

trying to do submerged arc welding of uranium. Submerged under flux. They were trying to weld big heavy plates of uranium.
Ed Bundridge came into the coffee room one day. He had taken
over some of Duncan's work while he was on vacation. This is
what he told me: "Hey, Montoya, you're always re-inventing the
wheel. Why don't you go try and see if you can weld some of
that uranium." I had done some submerged arc welding in the
shipyards. I remembered that they always emphasized the angle
of the electrode and the speed of the arc welder—the amperage
too.

I had watched Leo Christler try and weld some of that stuff
and he wasn't doing any good. They had two or three kinds of
fluxes that they were using with these plates, but he never cleaned
the plates properly. So I thought, hmm, and I took some of those
plates to electrochemistry and had them electroplate them, clean
them, you know. I would sand blast them in the hood and then
electro-cleaned. Then I would put them together and try to weld
them. Finally, what I did was take the electrodes and silver-plat-
ed them, the uranium rod that I was using. I did that because
it was real oxidized. I thought if I could get these parts really
clean, I might have something. Then I started working with the
fluxes, a little of this, a little of that. I weighed everything and
measured pretty close. I'd mix it real good and put the flux over
the plates. In one week I was welding uranium plates and it had
not been done before. I would weld a plate and I would take it
and sandblast away the flux that was stuck on. I would then take
it to electrochemistry again and have the plates cleaned real well
and then I would put another bead on there. Then I would take
the plate and cut it. They would do some photomicrographs of it
to see if I had any voids. They were perfect.

Staff members Bob Kyle, Ed Brundidge, Bob Kirby [a young
metallurgist], and Don Sandstrom were in my working group in
Sigma Building. Brundidge is dead and so is Kyle. He died of
lymphatic leukemia in Denver, where they took him. Brundidge
might have died of prostate cancer, I'm not sure. There was also

Jim Church, in charge of plastics, and Jim Gore in electrochemistry. Bob Kyle might have been in his mid forties. Ed Canton, a graphite machinist, was a little older than me and I was 40. All of these guys were in their forties. Then there was Frasier who got killed in the boiler, he was younger than me, mid-thirties. Hank Stroope. There was Boyer, a machinist. There was this guy we called Chango, but I can't recall his real name. He was also a graphite machinist. Then we had a janitor Biterbo Martinez, from Chimayó. Frankie Montoya, who died of cancer. There was a guy who died of cancer who worked in the plastics department; he had cancer up there in the head. I met him in the hall one day; he was Catholic, and he said, Ruben, look at me, pray for me. His name was Mundiger. Oh, there was Bob Vigil, the paratrooper's brother. He worked in the foundry and he died of cancer.

I don't think any of them lived to be 65 or 70. Maybe John Boyer did, he died while he was still working. I don't know if Brundidge retired before he died or not. Before I forget there was Jack La Motte, the *lambe* [suck-up, ass-kisser]. George Sweeney, Bob Osborne. There was another guy from Sigma who died but it was in a plane crash in Arizona. He was a pilot and was flying for Thanksgiving in bad weather. We all told him don't go. They hit a mountain; he killed himself and the whole family. I know there is a total of 48 men who died from Sigma.

I was one of those guys who kept track of everything and they didn't like it. I was the guy who instigated the technicians into keeping daily logbooks. They finally gave everybody logbooks because one time one of our bosses came into Sigma and said, now everybody is going to keep a logbook. I started doing it in survey and I still do it. I'll have a log about you coming here today.

MANUEL SALAZAR—*Property Auditor*

I was working for Zia and I got a job offer from the University of California [Lab manager]. They needed some people and there were a bunch of us at Zia. Zia wasn't as permanent as the University at the time, so we applied and got transferred. I started working as a property auditor. We controlled the location of equipment, property, and materials, gold and silver and platinum, osmium, precious metals. They were used for different shapes [material machined into different shapes] on the bomb. Some of it was coated with gold, silver, and osmium. We would audit the different groups for their use of the precious metals. We also investigated thefts of materials and equipment.

That got to be pretty bad. We had to fire quite a few people. This was in 1951. All kinds of things would turn up missing. Bulldozers! A contractor would rent a bulldozer to do a job and when he was finished he would take it with him to Kentucky or Tennessee. Sometimes we'd be told where it was taken and send out a man to locate it, or the FBI. We had a lot of portable drills missing, 65 I think it was. They were all numbered but gone. If people lost them they were charged for them. It was interesting ... .

I did this job for 31 years. One of the jobs in the office where I worked was to be responsible for the disposal of shapes and classified objects. We had shapes and equipment, lathes, etc., that were outdated and had to be buried; they couldn't be sold to the general public. They were sometimes contaminated with HE, high explosives and radiation. They were buried at Site-55. We had different pits for the classified subjects and shapes, parts of the bomb.

They were put in containers and placed in 100-foot wells, six feet in diameter. The wells were cut into the tuff rock, no casing. The stuff was placed in there and when it was full, they capped it with a six-foot concrete slab.

Some of that material was contaminated with tritium, one of

the worst. Most of the materials were in drums, in beryllium shapes. They had special vehicles that would place them in the pit and lower them real careful. I don't know if it's the contamination or the material that's being investigated now, regarding the health of some of the people who handled it.

It caught my eye, an article in the papers a while back about the government trying to compensate people who got sick from handling beryllium. I remember that I handled a lot of it. In fact, I broke this finger with one of the shapes that I was loading. There were two round shapes and as I was loading them into the back of the truck one swung into the other and caught my finger. They were small objects [he gestures 12 inches] but they must have weighed 100 pounds. Very dense. I went to the doctor and it was put into a cast for six weeks.

I was responsible for witnessing the destruction of DP West—doing away with the labs of DP East and West. It was done in 1980 or so. They took the whole thing and buried it.

They had big, deep pits across town at TA-55. We were there to physically verify that the material had been placed in the pit. It was highly contaminated and everything went. They were very careful and took precautions to remove all of the contamination they could. There are still areas that are contaminated today. They have about three fences around these areas.

When they were building the Los Alamos Inn where C and D buildings were there were some readings but I don't know how bad they were. The original buildings C and D were the bomb assembly buildings. Very interesting, I have seen … [pause, and tears well up] big changes, the old and the new.

I'm sorry I got emotional, I don't know why. But I loved working there. I made a good living. Everything we have we bought and paid for with our jobs in Los Alamos. I have two boys working for the labs now. They have good, well-paying jobs. Los Alamos has been a great thing for this area. I remember people used to sit around all day and did nothing. The economy has gone pretty well here. Everybody is buying new cars, and trucks, and new homes. Española's growing so much it's terrible.

They didn't know what the contamination would do, you know. They just didn't have the experience. I think that my Parkinson's comes from my involvement in the contaminated areas. I tried to take care of myself real well, but I think that it could be that I got it from there.

People favored the Laboratory at one time because of its role in stopping the war. It prevented a lot of people being killed. The bombs killed 200,000 people and that stopped the war. But … .

Of my 30 years on the job we did contamination removal roughly once a month. It varied according to the amount of material that was classified for disposal. We had to wear coveralls, gloves, and respirators a lot of times. Most of those people who worked in the dumpsite have died. These were the men who worked there permanently.

I knew them all: C. O. Martinez, Al Fernandez, Fermin Martinez, Bob Cox, who have all died. Almost all of them were exposed to the wind blowing the radiation, HE materials. You would breathe it, swallow it, you couldn't wear a mask all the time. The wind would kick up and would blow that contamination, a little each day and it would build up.

Most of them were due to cancer. There's no way of proving it. Many were dying at 75 on up, so they could argue that it was their time anyway. Like Celedonio O. Martinez, he was one of those who was in charge of the disposal site. He was from Chimayó.

I think the Lab is more careful now. OSHA [Occupational Safety and Health Administration] has a lot to do with it now. But, of course, a lot of it [contamination] is so old … .

They used to blow up a truck, for example, and I used to go and verify that it had been blown up. Then they would dig a big hole and bury it. There were accidents like those people who got blown up as they were sliding the HE material in the bed of the truck. It went off. It killed five or six, including Escolastico Martinez from Chimayó. They were going to take some material to burn but there were some materials that were highly explosive. They found out later that they had slid it across the truck bed and it sparked and blew and killed them all. I went to verify that the truck was destroyed. It was pretty well destroyed, I'll tell you. We buried the truck right at the site, at GMX 3, which was where they were working. This is one of the sites that doesn't exist anymore.

One of those wells was contaminated with tritium and I handled that classified burial. There were about six or seven wells and the tritium penetrated the wall of the next empty well, and that's what they were concerned with. They found some tritium where they dug the next well. It shouldn't have been. I wouldn't even stick around there. I'd give them the go ahead to put it in the wells and get out of there. The hell with witnessing. I said I did it even if I didn't; I got out of there.

The thing of it is, you grow up with it and you just don't take enough precaution. You can't see it, smell it, nothing. The only thing I ever contaminated were my socks and my shoes. I lost about 20 pair of shoes, and maybe 30-40 pair of socks in all that time. The shoes would be contaminated by the dust. Somebody would track in the stuff and you'd walk over it and when you went to the monitor you realized you needed new shoes to go home with.

I witnessed the material burial of three big accidents. Leo Guerin and Tom Burns were machining HE material. There must have been a drill that had a hole in it, with water in it to cool the machine while machining. It blew up the two of them completely.

Candelario Esquibel from La Puebla was cooking something in one of those sheltered areas and it blew up and he was squeezed through the fence. His brothers Ramon and Sam Esquibel survive him.

My mother's first cousin, Sevudeyo Lujan, was one of those who was blown up with the truck full of dynamite. He was one of the large group that I first mentioned. I knew all these men pretty well. They were the ones who did most of the hauling, and since I did the witnessing, I got to know them well. That was their job, disposal.

Mr. Lujan's son was one of the first to see where his father had been killed and squeezed like hamburger through the fence. It happened around 1955. I went out about a week after those men were blown up and you could still see the magpies and the ravens still digging out the flesh in the trees, you know.

PHIL SCHOFIELD—*Technician*

I was hired because I had long arms! There are two qualities they looked for, people who had an aptitude with their hands and could reach into the gloveboxes comfortably. Some of the gloves were just neoprene, others were a combination of rubber with lead, anywhere up to 30 mil thick.

With the 30-mil gloves it was very difficult to manipulate things. They were actually formed in a curved position, curled fingers. Depending on what stage in the game you were working, some of the gloves were very light for certain processes. You end up using a lot of hand tools, a lot of forceps, you get to where it's no real problem to manipulate.

Now, some of the finer stuff you learn to use forceps for, like picking up tiny screws if you're re-building a piece of equipment that you had to tear down to repair. If you're in 238 [plutonium] you have a lot of radiation that you need to be shielded from, whether it's gamma 239, or neutrons, depending on the material you're working with. Plutonium oxide is pretty mild stuff; it's mainly an alpha emitter. A piece of paper will stop an alpha particle. For that we could use the thin gloves, but when you work plutonium metal or PU 238, you want some lead in those gloves to stop all the gamma.

In DP Building 150 you actually had gloveboxes … if you think of a room there will be a set of gloveboxes and what we call the station with a conveyor, a little bucket that runs up and down a trolley that you can raise and lower and move from room to room. Maybe on each side of the room, it could also do it, depending on which room it was. We could move material back and forth. You had a series of gloveboxes on either side of the room and there would be something in the center as well. More gloveboxes. Take a dining room and put shelves on either side. In the middle is the dining room table. All our boxes are made out of stainless steel.

For working with the 238, because of the neutrons, they would have four-inch Plexiglas [to absorb the neutrons]. For our part we would have leaded glass windows and that was about the extent of the shielding that we had. It wasn't a big problem with oxide.

This was back before we had such luxuries as monitoring and red warning lights. That's one of the reasons that they built TA-55, because of the lack of safety, of ventilation. As a matter of fact, we were down in the basement of 150 building, a new line to do some production down there. We spent about a year building it when they told us to tear it all out. They were going to ship it all out to 55, which was still under construction. It didn't take too much to clean up the boxes to what was considered a safe level for us to physically crawl inside of them. We had to decontaminate them. They had been contaminated by the depleted uranium we'd had in there.

We wiped down the insides first, using regular cleaners, Fantastic, Versene, whatever. Then we took measurements until the readings were very low. We took off the windows and crawled inside the gloveboxes. We wore protective anti-C clothing but no facemasks or anything like that.

There is a picture of me and my co-workers sitting around eating a big, black cake. In the back you can see a transformer and it says PCBs and we're sitting there in our anti-C's eating cake. That was not uncommon. I remember when I first started, there were a number of incidences; I actually saw guys pull their gloves off, sit down, pour a cup of coffee, and eat a donut. They were probably going to have to work through lunch so they were grabbing a snack. Twice a day someone had to go up to the cafeteria and escort the ladies down with our coffee, tea, and hot chocolate. We drank it right there in the hot area. That way we didn't have to waste time changing clothes, etc. They supplied us with cigarettes. As long as you were working, you never had to buy cigarettes, if you were a smoker. Everybody used to carry these little plastic boxes that they kept crammed full. So we would eat and drink in that area.

There were a lot of us who knew what we were doing, particularly in later years, as we got more exposure and more things went on. We knew what we were doing was dangerous, we knew some of us were probably going to pay the ultimate price. But what could we do? This was our life, our career. We had worked ourselves into a box that we couldn't walk away from. We had families, we had to pay bills, and you pay the piper. We just couldn't quit and walk away.

I suspect the medical problems built up over the years, particularly at DP. It wasn't until probably the mid-80s that they got concerned about exposures, contamination, etc. At DP there were two times I got badly contaminated. I was drying some graphite. How I got contaminated, we have no idea. What I was doing was ball milling little sticks of spectrographic grade graphite. You'd put in some tungsten carbide balls and put it on a machine and shake it. Then you'd put it on a 425-mesh screen [425 holes per square inch], take a brush and work it. By the end of the day you were black from head to toe. We were using this very fine powder to make the fuel pellets for the breeder reactor. We used a half-facemask respirator but it seemed like that never worked as well as it should. At the end of the day you'd blow your nose and it would blow black. You'd wear two pairs of coveralls and you skin is black. The stuff was finer than powdered sugar, and would go everywhere. It was a dirty job. You're down the in basement, hidden in a corner, so that people didn't get into that dust.

We took turns whenever we needed more. You did it next to what we call an electro-dryer. That would dry the atmosphere, the air going into the gloveboxes, remove all the moisture. In that process you had to have less than ten parts per million oxygen and moisture in the air inside those gloveboxes. You want super dry air going in. Since that processed the air, maybe that was the source of the contamination. We'll never know.

Twice I was contaminated from head to toe with about 50R contamination. It was in my nose, in my hair. I had to go up and strip down. At that time there were no women working there, so you could walk from the lower buildings up to the showers buck naked. You go into the showers to get de-conned. They come in and scrub you down with Versene [a cleaning agent that neutralizes harmful metal ions], acetone.

I spent quite a while in the showers. The health physics monitors, people who keep tabs on this, came in and checked to see if there were any residual hot spots left. The hair was a real problem. Sometimes they chopped off a bunch of hair. Twice I had this happen. There were no nose swipes, no urine samples, no sending you to the body counter.

I was not alone. Often you see guys get it on their hands. At that time, it was a fact of life. We'd try Versene first or Lava, and then go to acetone next if it was stubborn. Most of this stuff was never recorded, never documented, it was just considered a common occurrence. This was in the mid to latter 70s.

It was the latter part of the 80s when I first noticed something was wrong. I was making a specialized isotope. Turns out because of the nature of the special isotope metal that I was working with—normally with plutonium you don't expect real high gamma, or real high neutron—I started having problems with very high gamma and neutron levels. At the end of the day they started to give me dosimeter pins that I would tape to my wrist each day. You could look in them and there was a little scale to read in there. The ones I was using had a one R scale. These were going off scale every day. I was using heavy leaded gloves, but by the end of the day, I had these extreme readings. I had about one Rad a day! They pegged out.

I started having some real concerns and Pablo [his RCT] did, too. He was a very conscientious man. At the end of the day the back of my hands were cherry red, like I had been out in the hottest sun. My hair started falling out. I went in to the supervisors and told them that I had a problem, I'm getting high gamma and a fairly significant level of neutron. My glovebox wasn't shielded at all for neutron.

They wouldn't believe me. They flat said no, that's not possible. You work in plutonium. I told them I didn't care what they said, this was what was happening. Finally Pablo went out and got a staff person and he literally grabbed them by the collar and took them to see the situation. He looked at the readings. The monitors did their survey and had marked with a grease pencil what the readings were. That did cause some concern, so they put a four-inch Plexiglas between me and everybody else. It didn't protect me at all!

There was an area on the other side of the glovebox where we did a lot of sampling, and they were afraid that those folks could get exposed, so they closed me off. The other problem was, I had some material, which I can't describe, but was stored in a lead pig. It was stored at my feet, underneath the glovebox. They did not want it down in the vault because it was considered too high gamma. I started having problems with my legs, from my ankles to my knees. Finally, when this project was over, it got to where if I got a little cut or bruise on the front part of my legs, it wouldn't heal. Dr. Williams had just started working for the Lab. He had been my children's pediatrician and was a man I knew and respected very much.

I went in to see him and he reviewed the medical history. He thought that radiation had damaged and destroyed a lot of blood vessels from my knees to my ankles. The only reason I can remember it so well is that he was recording it on a Dictaphone. I had heard of them but never seen one and I was fascinated. It had a little graphite cylinder and I watched as it cut the grooves in that cylinder.

But he basically couldn't do anything for me. He just said that it looked like I had received some radiation damage. All record of that day and the conversations are gone. Someone removed them from my medical file. I suspect that he got into trouble for that.

That's when things kind of first started. The latter part of the 80s I started having horrendous headaches, a lot of pain in my neck. Many weekends I would be in bed in pain. Finally I went to a doctor about it and he said the problem was my pillow. I must have bought two-dozen pillows trying to find one that would stop this. Then finally, I ran into a doctor from Lovelace who happened to be an expert in this area. He had seen these "hot box" injuries working with people from Eberline, people in the electronics industry who were using clean boxes with similar problems.

He knew exactly what it was, it's called head occipital cervical syndrome. It's where your head and your neck come together and everything gets damaged. I'm so tall that when I worked in gloveboxes, where a lot of people used little four-inch platforms to lift them up, I had to stoop and bend to work. I had to spread my legs and squat down sort of like a giraffe. If I stood up, I couldn't put my arms all the way in. The openings are standard on all boxes. They are narrower than my shoulders, so I had to cup my shoulders too. Years of this had created the damage.

I had been transferred out of the plant because of the headaches. It was determined that that was an ergonomic injury caused by my work. My doctor wrote a letter to the Lab and they were skeptical. They had a little guy from France or Belgium, their ergonomic specialist. He came to do an assessment and wrote a damning report. He wasn't there three minutes and said I can see the problem. Then they sent me to an orthopedic specialist for x-rays. I have never seen the report or the x-rays. All I know is that it confirmed what my doctor had said.

I was moved from inside the plant to what they call the operation center. Not long after that I developed a severe dermatitis on one arm and was actually hospitalized with it. Then the other arm, and then I started having a condition where the skin falls off my body. I swell up and it turns red and raw. It swells up so much it starts leaking. It's some kind of fluid that is being forced out through the swelling process. It looks like pine tree sap coming out of a tree. There are no obvious cuts or wounds, it just leaks out of my arms, my legs, my head. Some doctors suspect that it has to do with chemical exposure. Radiation may have played a part.

I don't deal with the Lab anymore. I was put on longterm disability in 1996. Before I left there were several doctors who told me off the record they suspected that all these health problems are related to my work at the Lab. But, they said they would never go on the record saying such a thing. They said it would be very, very difficult to prove that this was job related, except for the neck problems and the hearing loss [due to working in the pyro-chemistry lab with exceptionally loud pounding]. Workman's Compensation had to buy me hearing aids.

It didn't immediately become apparent, but one of the supervisors at that time told us we were "expendable assets." We knew where we stood. He couldn't give a damn about our safety. At one time, under the Cold War scenario, we were at war in a sense. Russia was busy developing more weapons, and we were busy doing the same thing. The number one goal was to produce more and more plutonium. That was the goal. Get as much pure stuff out the door for weapons development as possible. In a sense, this guy was telling the truth, we were expendable. Scary but honest. At that time, production of weapons material was more important than human life.

BEN ORTIZ—*Welder*

In 1976 I transferred to the vacuum section that was MP-11; the duties continued much the same, welding and the continued use of the solvents. I was more involved with a lot of oil vapors because these systems were bigger. I was in a section where we were responsible for the maintenance of the entire accelerator.

There were three tanks in this area of about five feet in diameter. When you would need to get into the tank area to replace instruments or a valve, or a physicist had some gear that had to get in there with some specific target for information from the beam, we would have to "let up" the system to air. That means to break vacuum. After you break vacuum, which takes roughly 30 minutes, you would go in and do the work. If you had a leak of any kind on a device or a valve, once the instruments detect it, they shut down the ion pumps.

Once you were ready to recover vacuum, we had huge mechanical pumps, WS Blowers. You have your mechanical pumps and then your blowers that worked together. Your mechanical pump might get you down to 10 microns [a millionth of a meter], and then the blower would kick on and take it down to one micron when the other blower would kick in. All this was to evacuate the air, the heat, moisture. A lot of the replacement devices that we would put in had epoxies, solvents. You're actually bringing a lot of garbage [water, air, any fine debris] out, too. The evacuation through the blower packages exhausts into the tunnel. The tunnel runs for about a half mile. It's smaller and the ceiling is lower. Everything down there is full of oil vapors, which are being exhausted through these blowers.

We didn't wear any respirators. For people like me, when our system became sensitized, minute exposures become a real problem. For the others without the problem, they were able to tolerate the exposures. I began to experience problems starting in '72 with my respiratory system: I had severe sore throats, sinus infections, really bad. I even got bronchial asthma. Also headaches. I would go to the doctors, lab doctors, and they treated my symptoms. I also went to private doctors because nothing seemed to help. I kept wondering what the heck was going on.

There was no diagnosis. They treated me like I had the flu or a cold. I did notice that the medication was ineffective. This went on and on from '72 up to '88. I went through a slew of doctors. The reason I went to so many doctors is because each time I would go to a new doctor they would keep repeating the same process, trying to treat the symptoms and not digging any deeper.

I really didn't begin to get some clues until about the early 80s. I was drawing some Freon out of a drum that was outside the building. The day was extremely hot and the drum had heated up. I was drawing five gallons out and right away it hit me, a terrible headache, and I got dizzy and nauseated. My eyes really got it too. This was my wake-up call that made me realize that the workplace was the enemy.

I'll jump ahead. After going to so many doctors, they did a work history on me at UNM [University of New Mexico]. After it was complete I felt very relieved that they finally found out what was going on. It had to make sense. Then I told the doctor, now that we finally have discovered what's wrong with me, cure me. Again, I was totally unaware of how long these toxins can remain in the system and cause trouble. She said that as far as she knew there was no cure. They made me an appointment with a man in San Francisco. I met with Dr. Cohen, the head of San Francisco General Hospital. He has been studying solvent exposures for many, many years. They did a lot of testing and he, in turn, referred me to Dr. Boller, who is a neurologist. The best advice Cohen could give me was to avoid further exposure. Avoid, avoid, avoid.

It is impossible to completely avoid that in this world. Once your body has become like a waste dump, I guess, anything sets it off. There has been some improvement, but there is still a long way to go.

I've been going to a private doctor up in Los Alamos and she does environmental medicine. Her name is Dr. Crone. The only good thing that I think came out of HSE-2 [a health group at the Lab] is that Dr. Shaw referred me to her. One of the times I went to him and my eyes were messed up, I was dizzy, with headaches, I was in terrible shape. I didn't even have to work with the materials anymore, just background levels, airborne, was enough to set me off, day in and day out.

I have a lot of skepticism about Lab doctors' opinions; there are many people who share that view. It doesn't have to be an illness, it can be an injury. LANL needs to hire occupational doctors and toxicologists to address the problems. They also need to hire unbiased people, if it's possible. The only one of their doctors back then who was certified as an occupational doctor was Shaw. I have been told through sources that he had no say-so. He was not the leading doctor up there. Nevertheless, I have to appreciate what he did for me, as far as directing me to Dr. Crone. She was able to direct me into the right path.

After three years that were considered the first phase of the accelerator, a lot of people moved out to other areas. I was one of the men who stayed back to run the furnace facility and continue brazing and welding. So I had many more years of contact than most of the others.

I have a letter from Senator Domenici giving me the argument that early mistakes were made because the war came first and there was not time to be concerned about health and safety issues. NIOSH [National Institute for Occupations Safety and Health] is telling me something else. They claim there was no reason why I should become sick. Maybe back in the 50s, but not the late 60s and into the 70s. NIOSH also said they have no way to oversee the Lab, but claim that they have all the information required to run a totally safe operation.

I know that at some of the meetings that I attended at NNMCC [Northern New Mexico Community College] with the CDC [Center for Disease Control] people a few years back, I gave a

156

lot of information to Larry Elliot and others and nothing ever came of it. Gilbert Sanchez [of San Ildefonso Pueblo] invited me. People from these organizations seemed sincerely concerned and asked me questions, but it never amounted to anything.

I guess I would have to say that I did enjoy my work up there. Many people do desire to work there, but as far as finding them [the Lab management] honorable people, I don't find them that at all. I would have thought for the betterment of everyone that they would have been more understanding. With all the knowledge that exists up there, I would have hoped that things could have been better. I was the loser. They ended my livelihood, there's no question about that.

ALEX SMITH—*Mercury Distiller*

Alex Smith

In late 1947, or the first part of 1948, I went home from work one evening and my face felt kind of funny. My wife said, what's wrong with your face? It's swelling up and it's red. It kept swelling and swelling and swelling. Finally my eyes went almost shut. The next day I went to the Q Building, the infirmary where the Health Division was located. I saw Dr. Whipple, who was the Group Leader. He said, "You're probably allergic to something. It's nothing serious, go home." I did and it went away. I went back to working with mercury and the same thing happened again. Saw him again and he sent me home again. This happened three or four times.

I didn't know what it was. I was a young fella and I didn't know what was causing it. But I lucked out. About the fourth or fifth time that it happened, Dr. Hardy was there in Q Building as a consultant. I think she was there from the New Jersey State Health Department. Of course, my face was all swelled up and I guess I looked pretty bad. She said right away, "Where do you work?" I said, "Well, I work at the chemical supply warehouse at K-Stock." She said, "Well what are your duties?" "I issue chemicals, laboratory glassware, lab supplies, and then if we're not too busy, I run a mercury still." She said, "You run a what?" I said, "I run a mercury still." "You mean that you distill mercury?" "Yes, I do." "Take me up there and show me." I took her up and showed her the little room and the still where we did the distillation. She said, "Oh my." She got in touch with the Group Leader, who was Harry Allen, and they shut it down. She checked the employees; one of them was Louis Caveglia.

He was in the same kind of shape but he never really reacted the way I did. But we were both full of it. We had it in our teeth, in our gums, it was terrible. She took us over to the old Army hospital. It was there by Ashley Pond and the Lodge. We both had blue lines around our teeth and gums. Our gums were bleeding. In fact, later on Lewis lost all his teeth. She told the doctors that that was the first place you could recognize it, that blue line around the gums. We both had mercury poisoning. I never worked with it again after that.

Bob Thompson was our supervisor at the time that I went to K-Stock. He was there before Louis and me and he did the same kind of work. He ran that still for probably a longer time than we did. Shortly after I got there, he left, went back to Texas, and died. He was a young man, a strapping 6' 5", 240-pounder. The first thing we heard was that he had died.

Dr. Hardy told them to check our urine every two weeks and watch us closer. They never did.

I was just a young guy, healthy, strong, and invincible, I thought. Louis and I talked about it a lot, and he told me, "Don't let them kid you, we got hurt and we got hurt bad. We're full of that stuff." Dr. Hardy had told us both on our trips over there to the hospital, I heard her say it, "It'll be with you for the rest of your life." I don't know if she meant the mercury or the effects. I think probably the effects because eventually, according to this publication, "Mercury Poisoning," she says in there that eventually your kidneys will dissipate it and it will work its way out. I'm not sure.

She's not sure either. There's a lot they don't know about mercury, believe me. She'll admit the fact that when she first came to Los Alamos she didn't know a heck of a lot about it either. She did know that it was bad stuff and that what we were doing was wrong, that we shouldn't have been distilling that stuff without any protection.

I went to work for the shops department in 1950 in the old foundry. I worked there for three years. I don't know about working conditions, but it was terrible. We didn't cast anything hot like they did in CMR. We cast mostly aluminum, lead, and a little copper. If I remember right, I think the whole inside of that foundry—it was a big building—was lined with asbestos to keep it from burning. There was fire all over. I stayed there three years and they shut it down. They moved it over to the big, new, shop which is TA-3. I went into the machine shop on the turret lathe. I worked for the shop's department until I retired in 1982. I enjoyed the work.

I didn't want to retire when I did but I started getting sick. I was only 56 years old but I started getting depressed. I have fought depression for a long time. Whether that's part of the mercury legacy or not, I don't know. I know that it can affect you that way. That's one of the things that it will do. The latter part of 1976 it started getting pretty rough. I had a friend there and he sent me to see a lady psychiatrist who was working with H-Division at the time. I was in bad shape. She sent me down to a hospital in Albuquerque called Vista Sandia. It was out there in the flats, this side of Albuquerque. It's no longer in existence.

I stayed as an outpatient to Dr. Kenneth Bull for about three years after that. Finally, I started feeling like I could do it, I could pull myself out of it, and I did. I can tell that it is still with me sometimes, but not as severe as it was in those days. I just couldn't work. I would look at a blueprint and all I could see was just lines, you know. They had a RIF [Reduction in Force] and I decided to take it. I discussed the fact that the mercury exposure was not on my records when I retired with one of the doctors who told me that we will look and see if we can find anything about it. The next time I went back to inquire he said, "There's nothing in the records about that." I told him about Louis losing all his teeth and he said that the only thing that he could find that refers to that mercury is that the Lab bought Louis a new set of false teeth! That's all the evidence that they had.

Surely they must have known how toxic it was. This was a National Laboratory. You have to read this pamphlet by Dr. Hardy. She says so much in these two brief articles. It enlightened me. She knew it was bad stuff at the time, but she didn't know how bad. Finding it on me and Louis seemed to spark her interest, and she started researching it. She came up with some information there that will knock your socks off.

After I read an article in *Parade Magazine* about how bad mercury poisoning is I got mad. I don't know if you recall a lawyer in Albuquerque named Leon Taylor? He was well known and I went to see him. I had in mind that I wanted to pursue this, despite the fact that I had no proof. He agreed to take my case. Let me look into it, he said. He called back a few days later and said,

"Alex, they've got us. The statute of limitations has got you." So I dismissed it then.

I've been suffering for years. I'm not exaggerating, I'm not complaining, but I hurt all over. I've lost both knees, my shoulder is shot, my back and my neck hurt, I think that stuff is in all my joints. I'll always believe that. I don't care what any doctor says. That stuff is in our bodies and it will stay there. I'm convinced of that just by the way I feel.

I'm the last remaining person who worked in that building who would know anything about it. They're all dead. But there was a man, Carl Buckland, who is the only living person who knows anything about this mercury deal, the one who did the , the head of that team. His letter to me [five pages, hand-written] is very detailed and he doesn't hold back any punches. In this letter he says that I can count on him for any testimony about the mercury still and its location. These are his exact words: "I would like to offer several comments and also to assure you that I will vouch for the validity of the correspondence available. You are welcome to provide my name to Representative Tom Udall as a reference concerning this matter … . In general terms, mercury is poisonous in many forms and combinations. Even the presence of a mercury vapor detector within the 1947-8 period suggests concern with this … ." It just confirms everything that I said.

I think they put us in harm's way for the ridiculous sum of $187 a month. Personally, I think they owe us big time. Louis can't collect his, he's dead. I don't know if I will either because I'm old, I'm seventy-five and how much longer I'll be around, I don't know. How I've lasted this long I don't know. It's amazing to me that I have made it this far. Maybe it's because it needed to be told. If it wasn't for me, nobody would have ever known about this mercury business. Nobody.

LOS ALAMOS REVISITED

Chapter Five

WHISTLEBLOWERS

Reading through all of LANL whistleblower Chuck Montaño's files elicited an overwhelming feeling of futility. Article after article, year after year, reporters were writing about the same controversies surrounding LANL: security breaches; mismanagement of funds; missing supplies; rip-offs; worker discrimination; impending Reductions in Force (RIFs, or layoffs); worker retaliation; individual and class-action lawsuits; toxic spills; toxic emissions; failure to meet deadlines; and around 2005, the impending privatization of the Lab by the Bechtel consortium.

The underlying analysis often used to contextualize these controversies, perhaps not quantifiable but in the end more damning, is the "culture of arrogance" believed to pervade not only LANL but the entire nuclear industry. Academics have written books about it—Peter Beacon Hale, Jake Kosek, and Joseph Masco—watchdog groups have filed suit over it, and disgruntled LANL employees have blogged about it: "LANL: The Rest of the Story" and "LANL: The Corporate Story," which were maintained from 2006 until 2010.

Former U.S. Energy Secretary Samuel Bodman told Congress in 2007 that "Bureaucratic issues are not at the heart of the problem. The heart of the problem is a cultural issue at Los Alamos … . It's arrogance. Arrogance of the chemists and physicists and engineers who work at Los Alamos and think they're above it all." And even former U.S. Senator Pete Domenici, the Lab's biggest supporter for many years, was quoted saying that the Lab has acquired "a reputation as being both dysfunctional and politically untouchable."

Some who have suffered the most from this culture are those classified as "whistleblowers," longtime LANL employees who because of their positions at the Lab as accountants, safety specialists, auditors, and quality assurance technicians became aware of the deep-seated problems at the Lab and attempted to alert their supervisors, and eventually, the public. They also helped found and participate in organizations and unions of Lab employees to protect their rights as workers. Three of these whistleblowers are profiled in this section: Chuck Montaño, Manny Trujillo, and Joe Gutierrez.

Chuck, Manny, and Joe were all born and raised in New Mexico, and because of their intelligence and hard work were able to go to college and rise in the hierarchy of the Lab into critical positions. Chuck became an auditor, Manny an engineering safety officer, and Joe worked in quality assurance. Chuck wrote a book, *Los Alamos: Secret Colony, Hidden Truths* [Desert Tortoise Publishing LLC, 2015], that documents his experiences. The book focuses on the common thread of arrogance of Lab management and the revolving-door culture among LANL, the DOE, the University of California, and Bechtel that prevents accountability. The name of the chapter that deals with the changeover from the non-profit management of the University to for-profit management of the consortium is "Lipstick on a Pig": Montaño says, "We went from bad to worse with the Bechtel led management." He knows there is never going to be internal LANL accountability; filing and litigating discrimination and grievance lawsuits costs workers too much, both financially and emotionally. Chuck, Joe, and Manny were all retaliated against—demoted, laid off, and isolated—but despite these hardships they continued their work as activists and organizers, and finally, truth-tellers. These are their stories.

CHUCK MONTAÑO

Chuck Montaño

I never thought about working at Los Alamos. My dad worked up there in construction. He built houses on Barranca Mesa and in White Rock. I used to go with him as a kid when I was in high school. He used to contract, beyond his regular 40-hour week, doing the prep work on the houses for plastering. I was his laborer and we'd do this on weekends.

That was my initial exposure to Los Alamos, no pun intended. My dad always felt that the people up there were wealthy. Everyone did, and in fact, they are. They would buy things that you couldn't get on the hill. They would buy manure for their lawns, so my dad had an old dump truck and we would go to Taos and load it by hand and then drive it up the hill, climbing at about five miles an hour. We would go door to door asking if people wanted to buy manure. That was my other early experience with Los Alamos, selling manure. The people were nice. I was always cognizant of the fact that they were all well-educated and affluent, even then. They had horses, nicely manicured lawns. Their homes seemed immense to me. The reality is that the vast majority of them are just like everybody else, they work for a living. Not all of them were born with silver spoons in their mouths. A lot of them have worked very hard for what they have.

I knew nothing about the Lab, and the only reason I ended up working there was because when I was at New Mexico Highlands one of my roommates was from Los Alamos and he happened to be Hispanic. His name was Michael Gallegos. His dad worked for Zia and that's how Michael ended up working there. His parents were from La Madera, one of the rural communities in northern New Mexico, and Los Alamos offered jobs to people like this.

I do remember him telling me stories that were quite disturbing about the way he was treated while he was in school in Los Alamos. There was a lot of racism. There was a lack of understanding and empathy in the early years for the Hispanic and Native populations. The women were brought in to do the menial work, like cleaning houses. The men who were hired did construction and janitorial work. There was a real big division in terms of the jobs that people could get and where they could live. This is all documented in a book by Peter Bacon Hales called *Atomic Spaces*.

I applied and about a month went by and Michael called and asked whether I had been called in for an interview. I told him I hadn't and he was concerned because they were almost finished with the process. He encouraged me to call Dimas Chavez, the Equal Employment Officer and ask him if he could look into it. At the time the Lab had an EEOC [Equal Employment Opportunity Commission] function that was more of an advocacy role, compared to now where all they do is talk about how we should all be friends. The advocacy is gone now. Then they asked the question about why the Lab wasn't hiring qualified minorities in greater numbers.

Within a couple of days I got a call to go for an interview. I went in and got the job. It turned out that the man who I worked for, Whitey Thorpe, was a wonderful man. I got real close to him. He died two or three years later of cancer. He was a heavy smoker. I used to drive him to Albuquerque for his chemotherapy. It was a heart-wrenching experience. Experiences like that remind me we're all human. It's crazy that we spend so much time and effort fighting one another, when in the end the pain is just the same. It still affects me when I think about him.

He was working in the nuclear material safeguards area. That group kept track of all the nuclear materials in the Lab: where they were located, the quantity, the movements. When I went to work at the Lab, that's where I started. Instead of counting dollars and cents, you're counting grams of plutonium and uranium.

I did that for three years. Right after Whitey passed away I left. I got another job in the accounting division. I started there in systems development. That was my transition into this kind of work. I had been doing some of that in the safeguard area, a tracking system for the movements of the nuclear materials. So when I moved over they were in the midst of a major system revamping all of their processes.

RIFS: REDUCTION IN FORCE

It was in 1995, the RIFs (Reduction in Force) had already been announced. Prior to that I had been involved with the Hispanic Roundtable, which was a group of Lab employees who had basically formed an underground union. In 1992, under Sig Hecker [Lab director from 1986 to 1997], the Lab had disbanded all the special emphasis groups, the minority groups. They were all advocating for change, so management decided the easiest way to deal with the pressure was to disband them. We were no longer allowed to organize and meet on Lab premises.

Then the Hispanic Roundtable was formed. I was invited to get involved largely because my advocacy at the schools was known [Montaño was instrumental in getting a racist mural at the high school redone]. Others may have known about the

Safeway dispute [Montaño's wife filed a sexual harassment suit against the chain], so they may have thought that I would be willing to speak out. What I saw at the meetings was a lot of complaining, but no one seemed prepared to take it to the next level, and that was to figure out what to do about it.

The Department of Energy had already decided to move the pit production that was done at Rocky Flats to Los Alamos. They needed to get buy-in from the community because as late as 1992, both Sig Hecker and his Deputy, Jim Jackson, had been quoted in the media as saying that under no circumstances would they ever support the Lab taking over pit production. The reason was simple. The Los Alamos National Laboratory was a basic Research and Development facility, not a production facility. That's why the University of California had always managed it. They saw it as falling within their academic mission. It was basic science. If the pit production were moved here, it would be a lot harder to defend that position and definition of the mission.

In 1994 the DOE was looking for ways to streamline the whole complex. There were all of these rumors running rampant about downsizing and budget cuts. That was used by the DOE and the political establishment as leverage to change the University and Lab's view of the pit production. If you don't comply, the big pot of money will shrink. Lots of money will have to be spent on pit production to upgrade facilities, build infrastructure, and that will keep the institution going into the foreseeable future. Without pit production, budgets will shrink dramatically.

So suddenly we see a flip-flop in the stated views of the higher-ups. It will not really be a production effort, it will be the stockpile stewardship program. We are not going to be looking to build new weapons systems, we are going to be involved in maintaining the existing stockpile. The University, of course, bought into that. They claimed it was a survival decision, the only way to maintain the economic viability of the institution at its current size. They also argued that the country had nowhere else to go. They didn't have the facilities or the expertise anywhere else. That decision had already been made in 1994. They showed an increase in their budget based on this decision. The powers that be needed to garner buy-in from the community. It's a common tactic. It was used during the Manhattan Project days. They would go out into the community and meet with the community leaders, stroke them a little, give them a tour of the facility, give them some inside perspective, make them feel like they are a part of the inside rather than the outside, and you get more support for what you want to accomplish.

In early 1995 they announced that not only were they going to go through with a downsizing exercise in '95, but they were also going to have one in '96 and in '97. The Defense Conversion Act was one the Congress passed to help the DOE downsize throughout its facilities. But the downsizing was occurring at the production sites. Pantex was going to be downsized dramatically. The need for new weapons systems wasn't there. The downsizing was due at Hanford where we didn't need to produce more plutonium, at Oak Ridge where you didn't need more uranium, etc. All this was on the drawing board, but not at Los Alamos and not at Livermore. It wasn't in the cards.

In 1992 and 1993 the Lab had offered early retirement incentives. Guess what they had done in those same years? Hired nearly a thousand people. We had these numbers. Why were they all of a sudden talking about a layoff, when they had been on a hiring binge up to that point? They knew they had to replace some of those early retirees because they were gearing up for the Stockpile Stewardship program. So now in '95 they are talking layoffs. As '95 progresses into the summer, the talk of layoffs continues. I have now been identified as a spokesman by the media. We're holding our Roundtable meetings at the United Church in Los Alamos. All of a sudden there is less and less room in that conference room. More and more people are coming. Many of the new people aren't Hispanic.

Now we ask whether we can use the church proper for our meetings. It's standing room only and half are Anglo. It is no longer a Hispanic advocacy organization, it is now a labor organization. Why do they come to us? They are afraid because they are getting indicators that they may be fired. These are people with 10, 15, 20 years of service. Many are at the tail end of their careers and they know that this is the end of the game for them if they lose this job. These are people who over the course of their careers have pissed off somebody. They know they are vulnerable, and have nowhere else to turn. We are now speaking a broader language of fairness and equity. We're talking about job protection for every variety and color of worker.

In October 1995, we formally incorporated as CLER, Citizens for LANL Employee Rights. It evolved from the Hispanic Roundtable of Los Alamos. We approached Domenici and he went public and said there is no budget crunch projected. Now the Lab has to look for another reason and Sig Heckler is looking pretty foolish. So they call it a workforce restructuring initiative. We need to change the ratio of technical vs. support staff, that's the reason.

They were committed from the top. We're talking about 55 years of arrogance. It was in November of 1995 that the layoffs hit. The total number of layoffs, including contractors, approached one thousand. We exposed the fact that the Lab wasn't having a fiscal crisis. We saw this primarily as an excuse to clean house and get rid of troublemakers. The beauty of this for the Lab was that it wasn't even going to come out of their budget. The Defense Conversion Act was going to pay for it all. The Congress had a separate pot of money to cover these expenses.

That put a temporary halt to the layoffs due in June and July and a separation plan was offered. The incentive was you get $20,000 severance or whatever you were due under the severance policy, whichever is more. Rather than leaving it up to managers as to who left, we wanted people who were willing to leave to volunteer.

Over five hundred people volunteered to leave. The Lab had projected that approximately 500 regular fulltime employees would have to go. It was perfect, except the Lab said it reserved the right to pick and choose which of these it would allow to go. Then if it still had to let more go involuntarily, it would do that. They allowed about half of the 500 to go. Even though the Lab had been given an opportunity to avoid involuntary separation, they still decided to go with it. They are bound and determined. They are not going to blow the chance to clean house without interference. Maybe they're too old and slowing down, maybe they have medical problems and miss too much work. Maybe they are complaining about health and safety, or racial diversity.

In September people got their notices and you had thirty days to try and find something else at the Labs or you were out the door. CLER had been working with Morty Simon and Carol Oppenheimer, lawyers from Santa Fe. Carol and Morty were stunned with the way the workers were being treated. The stories they were hearing … they started attending some of our meetings and people were hungry for them to listen to their stories as to why they had been targeted. People who had been there 20 years were being targeted and they were scared to death. They had mortgages to pay, others had medical bills.

Carol and Morty, being the kind of people that they are, probably let their hearts get the better of them. Thank God we have a few attorneys left like that. They said we can't just sit back, we need to try and stop this layoff. They filed for a RIF injunction. We went to court, a three-day hearing before Judge Hall, in the First Judicial Court. The media was there daily. We were the headline news in that period. We were going up against an institution that had never lost a labor case, ever. I was very actively lobbying behind the scenes. They knew now that I was the leader of a large organization and treated me accordingly. Politicians were starting to pay attention.

We won the injunction hearing. People were shocked—it made national news. We stopped the layoffs. The Lab then appealed it to the state Supreme Court. The court heard the arguments, two days before Thanksgiving. They could have had the compassion and the heart to have waited until after the holiday to render their decision but no … the court rushed that decision and on Thanksgiving eve they announced that they had overturned the injunction.

The argument that the Lab used was that there would be no irreparable harm done to the workers if the RIF was allowed to go forward because the workers still had the option of suing. The Lab, however, could suffer harm by delaying the layoffs because their tight budget situation would be exacerbated. Now they were back to the budget argument.

The people got laid off and the media continued to follow the story because now we were organizing into a group lawsuit. It was obvious that now the fight was to try to reimburse or remedy people's loss of their jobs. The next phase of the fight was going to be reinstatement, because under the Defense Conversion Act there were two important provisions that the Lab ignored. The first said that people who were laid off under the restructuring of the DOE complex were entitled to medical benefits for two years. The Lab did not offer any benefits. Senator Jeff Bingaman helped us with this. We were very disheartened that our Congressional delegation did nothing to prevent the layoffs. Bill Richardson was the worst. He did absolutely nothing, even after many appeals.

In April of 1997 we went to court. We filed a group complaint with the Office of Federal Contract Compliance [OFFCP]; discrimination based on ethnicity. That's where you have to go when you're dealing with a federal contractor. If you want to file a claim based on age discrimination you have to go with the EEOC. We did that too. We had several different fronts activated. We had the political front, the media front, the OFFCP, the EEOC, and we had a group lawsuit. From the original 200 members of CLER we now separated the wheat from the chaff and looked to see who was ready to put their money up and do the fundraising. We ended up with 102 people who wanted to go to the mat. To start the process, we needed two thousand dollars from each one. On top of that we raised three hundred thousand selling raffles. That still wasn't enough. The Lab spent about seven million fighting us. Our half a million wasn't enough to cover Carol and Morty's expenses.

The result was that we got a favorable determination leading up to the court hearing, in April of 1997. We had a formal lawsuit with over 100 plaintiffs. The Lab hired the Rodey firm, the largest in New Mexico. They filed motion after motion to water down the suit. The costs were skyrocketing. The strategy was to make it as costly as possible for us since we had limited resources. My job was to keep people motivated in the face of this opposition and flagging spirits. The Lab was using an army of spin-doctors in public affairs and we were still trumping them in terms of our stories in the press.

We went to trial and it lasted an entire month. Even Judge Hall felt a lot of sympathy for us. The Lab didn't want to litigate this case in Santa Fe, so they did it in Albuquerque. The jurors were recent arrivals to New Mexico and had no historical perspective on the issues. A lot of them were migrants and may have lost their jobs where they lived before, so their sensitivity to the issues could be keen. Or just the opposite, they might have felt that I suffered through it, now why can't you? The case wasn't framed around the discrimination but around the contract employment law. Hall asked for five plaintiffs: the Lab picked five who they saw as having trouble with their work records and we picked five who were the strongest. We had a former Commander of the Navy, a weapons designer, etc.

They put the ten names in a hat and the judge drew five names out. Three of the five were theirs and two were our people. We ended up with four Hispanics and one Anglo, Henry Atwater. In the end four of the five lead plaintiffs lost but Henry Atwater was awarded $482,000.

The Lab immediately appealed. Henry threw his award in the pot. He was devastated and heart-broken that he was the only one who prevailed. That jury decision was an absolute disgrace. The Lab got even more than they could have dreamed from this jury. Leading up to the decision it seemed to me that the Lab lawyers were feeling pretty discouraged. Believe it or not, Judge Hall went into his chambers and cried after the decision came down.

In the meantime, we already had the legislators from California who had said we are going out to New Mexico to see what is going on. They sent out a scout and he was struck by the "disconnect" that he observed there. They decided to convene a hearing in May of 1998. This and the presidential visit of Bill Clinton really made the difference. These two events were responsible for prompting the Lab to settle. On the eve of our going out, the Lab had already notified us that they were going to settle.

Five CLER members were involved in the negotiations. They were tough negotiations and the Lab broke them off once. The Lab offered the RIFs five thousand dollars apiece and no attorney's fees; they were that arrogant. These are bullies and they don't respond to appeals of reason. Finally, though, every one of the 102 workers averaged between $20-$35,000. They got the two-year health coverage as well. It wasn't a full remedy, but it was vindication. It was unheard of to go to trial, lose, and then still have a settlement.

The Lab didn't just settle, it was an enormous battle. In the end, I think people look back gratefully to CLER. While some may not have supported us at the time, I think in retrospect, many have benefited.

MANNY TRUJILLO

Manny Trujillo

[The breakdown of the telecommunications industry in the early 1980s, within which he had been working, prompted Manny Trujillo to apply at Los Alamos.]

Here's the Laboratory that's been in our backyard all this time, and I never even considered working there when I was getting my education. It would have been the last place I would have considered working. But when all this transpired with Contel I thought seriously about it for the first time. I thought, in fact, that it would be a great opportunity for me to excel and move up in the rankings of the work structure there. I thought I had something to contribute.

In fact, I found it just the opposite. I worked in outside industry for so long that I felt that my work ethics were focused on meeting deadlines and getting things done in an efficient manner. I found that was very different than the expectations at the Laboratory. Of course, the Lab was a not-for-profit organization.

I went into the design engineering division and I started

working at a satellite engineering office for the Meson Facility at LANC (Los Alamos Neutron Center). That's where the beam and the accelerator is. At that time there was a lot of money coming in from Washington for construction. I was the electrical engineer on the team. We had another person who was mechanical, another who was structural, and two who did the drafting.

At that time the accelerator was already built, but there were other functional facilities that needed to be built that would support the beam. Here I was, all geared up to do the work, and I found out, as Joe Gutierrez did, that I was asked not to finish things so promptly, kind of hold back in completing things. It was hard, so what I ended up doing to deal with it was that I finished my projects and then pigeon-holed them until they required them. I didn't want to jeopardize others' positions and make waves, so I figured if I can just complete my work and keep it in a holding pattern until it is requested, then this was the best way of dealing with the situation.

I stayed there from 1985 until 1988, about three years. The Lab is famous for reorganizing and 1988 was the first one that I went through. We got moved to another facility called the Pajarito School. It's a leased facility, one that the Lab leases from the county. They decided that they wanted to keep the whole engineering division together in one facility and basically, by 1988, things were toning down at LANC so it was appropriate to consolidate people in a central location. But I already knew what to expect at this new location, work ethic wise.

Interestingly enough, the engineering division was one division where there were quite a few Hispanics. In fact, many of them had graduated from New Mexico State, my alma mater. The two people who hired me, the group and deputy group leaders, were both from New Mexico State. It's another indication of the tightness of the Laboratory. If you know people and they know you, you get in. If you don't, forget it.

Our division was unique in that it contained a sizable number of Hispanic professionals. I didn't see that in other divisions at the Laboratory. It was really nice working in that environment.

Seeing the advancement of Hispanics over the years to positions of group and deputy group leaders—it was appealing. I started applying for positions, not only in the engineering division but outside because there were other areas where I thought I could be productive as well. It was one excuse after another, not being able to get a position. I started to wonder, hey, what's going on here? I thought once you got into the Lab and you were productive, you were doing a quality job, you could move up. I had developed experience in a variety of areas. As an engineer, you were sent to a variety of different sites to do many different projects. You got to know the areas and the people and their facility.

Finally, my persistence paid off when I got to be Form B, which is one way of being sent to another division, although you're still wearing the division hat of engineering. Basically what I was doing was bringing in money to the division by being Form B, which was picking up my expenses because I was doing work for them. This is like sub-contracting within an environment at the Lab. This was 1991-2, and that was when funding was coming in very heavily for Star Wars. I got involved with laser optics and the instrumentation that was being used in Desert Storm. I wasn't involved directly with the weaponry but in the support systems and the engineering work necessary to support those activities.

That lasted for about two and a half years. Then came the big thing at the Lab, which really ruffled some feathers. This was the Tiger Team's arrival. That really impacted on the Lab's ability to continue doing what it had always done. The Tiger Team dealt with environment, safety, and health. They started scrutinizing certain areas of Laboratory work to see if things were being done in an environmentally sound way.

Environmental health issues were becoming important all over the country, and DOE had facilities that were going to be closed. It was the end of the Cold War. It might have actually been a [Dick] Cheney legacy because he was very much involved in closing down DOD sites. Part of that closing had to do with clean-up, of course.

The mentality and the culture that had existed at the Laboratory was suddenly being jeopardized because, all of a sudden, size was no longer a priority. It had to deal with the actual cleaning up of the facility, making it sound environmentally, as well as in terms of safety and health. Of course, the money was now flowing into these areas. The scientists and the Laboratory management were very much at risk of losing the funding for their mission, which was nuclear weapons. It really affected the funding for those weapons programs. There was a lot of resistance to all this. Don't mess with us, we are the crown jewel facility of the country and we are here to sustain the nuclear mission and we are not to be impeded in any way. Suddenly a monkey wrench was being thrown in the works and we were being asked to divert our whole focus toward making sure we do things right as far as safety, health, and the environment.

The Lab recognized that the Tiger Team meant business. They were found deficient in a large number of areas, some 80,000 deficiencies as I recall. There were some 2,000 sites that were recognized as needing to be cleaned up. All of a sudden DOE and Lab management saw that lots of dollars were going to be needed to achieve all of this. That meant fewer funds for weapons and Research and Development.

Lo and behold, I was asked to be the engineering division safety officer for my division. That was because of my OSHA [Occupational Safety and Health Administration] background in outside industry. OSHA came into outside industry a lot earlier, like in the early 70s, so I had training and experience with them in terms of electrical standards. The division also needed somebody who could deal with the questions and answers to those in the Tiger Team. I was asked to relieve myself from Form B and come back to the division in this new role.

Again, I wanted to do what was right. In doing so, I got into trouble because I started seeing that management and scientists were trying to divert themselves from doing the right thing. As an S and H [safety and health] officer I had to call it as I saw it. I stepped on a lot of toes.

After the initial impact of the Tiger Team, after they left, the studies started to surface. The first thing that came up was how do we deal with all the assessments that were made. How do we prioritize them and which are most critical? A lot of money was spent just trying to do that much. How do we estimate the cost of all of this? That was done and those estimates were high, so those estimates could go to Washington and our political leaders who sit on committees that fund the Laboratory could now use these studies to justify their requests for funding. It will cost this much to clean up chemicals, it will cost this much for the electrical upgrade, security upgrades, fire upgrades, etc.

The money all went down the tubes. Like I said, very little got done. The Citizen's Advisory Board came about to try and oversee what was being done. We were very vocal, and because of our outspoken behavior we were disbanded. I got on the Board after I was RIF'ed [Reduction in Force] in 1995. I think my removal was based on my having been very vocal and visible in trying to address the problems that I thought were significant. In 1993, Sig Hecker [Lab director from 1986 to 1997] went through a reorganization. I saw that many of my Hispanic friends who were twenty-year veterans, who had struggled to achieve positions as group leaders, were being demoted. Hecker's claim was that he was trying to streamline management, fewer at the top, and achieve greater efficiency. That reorganization cut at the fiber of a lot of Hispanic professionals. In practical terms it meant that key people were suddenly demoted. It caught my eye as well as Joe Gutierrez, and Chuck [Montaño] and others. It seemed to hit the Hispanic work force most directly. We saw that the glass ceiling was being lowered dramatically.

About 195 UC [University of California] employees were RIF'ed. Initially there were more—there might have been as many as 500—but you have a 60-day grace period to find other employment within the Lab. I applied for three or four other positions that I was qualified for, but they kept their hands off. A blacklist had gone out.

The Hispanic Leadership Team was initially five people, but we started having meetings with other employees when the RIF was more visibly coming, around April, May, and June of 1995. At that time we started getting others involved and we changed our name to the Hispanic Roundtable. There were quite a few of us then because of the concern of being RIF'ed. We had continued to be very vocal during those months about what we saw was going on at the Laboratory. There were town hall meetings that were being held in Española, Pojoaque, and Los Alamos. We were still under the Lab's employ but were very vocal about expressing our views on the issues. This gave them even more incentive to retaliate and get more people on the RIF list.

I hope that the struggles that we went through will create a legacy that will support our next generation. That was basically our beginning premise when the five of us began. We met with Hecker and he asked, point blank, what is it that you guys want? He seemed to think that it was about individual pay-offs. I got a little offended and told him, no, we don't want anything specifically for ourselves. What we want is to insure that there is an institution at this Laboratory that will provide an equitable work place for our children. We want to be able to look forward to a bright future for them here at the Laboratory. We don't want doors slammed in their faces; they need to have equal opportunity to excel and flourish in their working lives. We know for us it is too late, but we don't want what's been going on here for over 50 years to continue to plague their futures. We don't want them to fall into the same boat that we find ourselves in. This Lab must become inclusive and provide the opportunities, not to just a selected few but to everyone. That's what we want.

I came back to the Lab in 1998 and became involved in union organizing. I'm still a target but there are some shields there that provide protection so the bullets bounce off. The shields are that you're visible, you're vocal. The minute you let your guard down, that's when the bullets can do some damage. Being visible means we are still very actively engaged with the political leaders, both here and in California. That provides a shield. We are still very much in the forefront with the media. Being a board member of University Professional and Technical Employees (UPTE) provides a shield. Here we are promoting what we always wanted, an instrument or a mechanism within the Laboratory, where employees can have a sounding board, a place where they can voice their concerns without fear of retaliation.

UPTE originally started at Livermore [the laboratory in California]. It is now very strong within the UC campuses in California. What promoted that was the fact that UC was under a law called the Higher Education Employment Relations Act (HERA). It was not granted to Los Alamos employees because we were not in California. That was what negated Los Alamos employees from having the protection of a law like that. We didn't find that out until we were in the throes of battle with the Laboratory. We found out that New Mexico labor law did not protect because they saw us as UC employees. California law didn't protect us because, in their eyes, we were New Mexico residents, not Californians. We were in a dire predicament. We didn't have any legal protection from the Laboratory and its management. They knew it full well. That's why they were able to get away with a lot of things in the past. If it hadn't been for our interaction with the legislative body in California, we'd still be in the same situation. In January of 2000, HERA became very inclusive as a result of some legislation and changes of wording in the act. Now, for the first time, we are under the protection of the State of California.

UPTE is affiliated with the Communication Workers of America (CWA). CWA is the umbrella organization under which we operate. Finally we have control of our destiny and if we don't take advantage of it, it won't be through anyone's fault but our own. This is the opportunity that we've been waiting for.

Unfortunately, the culture of reprisal, that behavior is still imbedded in the Laboratory. The reason is you still have people in management from the old regime. Until those things start eroding, I don't think there will be much of a change in the culture and mentality of the Lab. The reprisals have become more subtle, and that's something that we must be aware of. Employees have seen the results of speaking out and it will take a lot of persuasion to change their minds and convince them that a union can protect them from this behavior. Even right now, despite the efforts that we are mounting in order to get UPTE on its feet, there is resistance and there are reprisals. We see it.

I tell you, when you can establish common ground … I think this was one of the reasons for CLER's success [Citizens for LANL Employee Rights]. We established common ground not only with Hispanic issues, but all of a sudden we became inclusive of others. That common ground created a common bond. It was amazing to hear these members who joined CLER. Many of them were taught when they first came to the Lab, you don't want to go down to the Valley or associate at all. It's dangerous, etc. They had a certain fear instilled in them without knowing the reality. They find themselves in a cloistered community and they don't know any better.

When they got involved with us and started coming down here for parties and things, they started getting to know us as people. They kept saying this is great, this is the most fun we've ever had in New Mexico! Here we are all suffering through the RIF, you know, but managing to have a good time in spite of it. They suddenly realize there's another world out there and it's terrific! That to me was an eye opener. All of a sudden you saw these barriers go down, and people enjoying one another, discussing things and having mutual agreements and disagreements in a respectful way. It was great. We're hoping that those same people that are out there now, and I know they are, are telling others how great this community of ours is.

When I started being vocal and trying to get things going, my dad mentioned to me, "I need to remind you about your grand-pa." I asked him what he meant. He told me that back when my grandpa was working at the first sawmill in Santa Fe, which was in Santa Fe Canyon, the employees were asking management for a better rate of pay. The workers came to my grandpa and asked him if he would go and talk to the manager for them. They said they'd stand behind him and if need be, strike. My grandpa took them at their word and went and asked for a higher wage for everyone. The manager said no and said if he didn't like things he could leave. My grandpa picked up his lunch box and left thinking they would all follow. They didn't budge! So my dad's advice to me is, make sure you have the workers' support before you do anything extreme! (laughter)

JOE GUTIERREZ

Joe Gutierrez

[Joe got his degree in civil engineering and worked in the nuclear power industry in the south before going to work at Los Alamos.]

I didn't really pursue getting a job in Los Alamos very aggressively. What happened was a friend of my father-in-law happened to learn of my background and my interest in coming back to New Mexico. Through him I had access to the Lab. I submitted a resume and in 1989 I was asked to consider working at Los Alamos. My actual offer came on Good Friday. By April 28th we drove into the area and I started on May 1st.

I was a standards coordinator in what was then called the Engineering Division. What that meant was that the Lab had been attempting to put together a standards program and resurrect one that had been in place in the past: how to design structures, how to maintain operations, electrical standards, etc. I was hired specifically to update and upgrade the program, and put the standards in the computer and get the operation computerized. Utilize informational technology to update and upgrade. This was over the entire Lab.

That's when I got an initial sense about the safety issues. Part of the task was to develop and upgrade the electrical standards. There was a lot of concern about some of the field conditions perhaps not being as safe as they should be. We needed to assure that people had the training and awareness of how you made certain connections. You would shut down certain systems in a certain way before you worked on them to eliminate any chance of electrocution. These concerns were significant to a lot of people at the Lab, particularly the engineers who knew the conditions in the field. One man in particular gave me a black binder of issues that he had collected in areas that he felt needed some scrutiny.

One of the really frustrating things here at the Lab is that we go through a reorganization every few years. They were reorganizing the engineering division and as a result of that process people were also retiring. There was little continuity between the retirees and the new people coming in. So I ended up reinventing the wheel.

Unfortunately, what had been done had not been captured. It wasn't documented either in drawings or in the way of instructions. It wasn't captured in the way of training or making people aware of what the program was. People would retire without passing along information. The new people would have to relearn. I have the perspective of one who has come from industry. When these things happen in industry, it's a planned event. They know that somebody's going to be leaving a few years on and they start grooming people into those positions.

The other problem was that you didn't have a clear line of communication to a senior manager. Since I was in charge of the standards program they came to me, thinking that I could help rectify some of these problems. The issues fell on deaf ears. My management was unresponsive. In one particular meeting I had with my manager he said we really wanted you here for your credentials. We can tell people we have a real expert but we really don't want you to push too hard. Then in 1990, a year after I had arrived, my immediate supervisor came in and told me that I needed to slow down, you're pushing too hard. I asked him what he meant by slow down. He said, "You're attempting to do too much too fast, the system can't handle it." I said, "Gee, I haven't even begun to do what I hoped to do, I was just revving up." I dismissed it and thought that maybe I was being too aggressive in some sense. I tried to reflect about it. Several months passed and he came back and repeated the same warning. This began to tell me that my method of work wasn't really compatible with theirs.

In 1991 I was called into my supervisor's office and he said that they were hearing complaints about me. He said, "Some people in our division and others don't appreciate the way you are communicating and not communicating." I said, "Let me try and understand this. Can you tell me what the issue is?" He said, "No, you're too good. You probably know who is complaining and we don't want you retaliating against him." I said. "I don't care about getting names, I just want to know the nature of the complaint." He said. "Try and locate yourself somewhere else in the Lab. We basically don't want you in this division."

The DOE Tiger Team was a collection of inspectors who were coming in to examine the overall operation of Los Alamos. I went ahead and relocated in the area that was going to respond to the Tiger Team. It worked well for me. I was able to provide input to the team leader and used my experience to help predict what the Tiger Team was going to see. I helped analyze which areas were going to be real issues and which were not and how to establish priorities and sequence the work so that we were prepared when they came.

Have things improved since the Tiger Team? It's a mixed bag—certainly some things have gotten better. If nothing else there's a greater awareness of worker safety. There's also a little more latitude for the worker to speak out, not what it needs to be but better than what it was. There is still a lot of fear of retaliation. People who complain can still lose their jobs or get moved elsewhere, thereby losing the seniority they may have accrued over a period of time.

In mid-'96 I saw an article in the paper where Jim Jackson, Assistant Director of the Lab, is quoted as saying that he knows that the Lab is in compliance with 31 of the 33 stacks in the Lab that emit radionuclides. The quality assurance program is alive and well. This happens to be one of my strong suits. I had routinely audited that area and had found serious problems.

The quality assurance program is directed to a series of managerial areas—design control, maintenance, document control, all the managerial tools to keep track of operations and their status. Jackson made this statement in June and in July there was an accident. A student had been shocked pretty badly but recovered. That forced the Director to close down the Lab for a day to make people more aware of the problems. The stand-down comes from the military; it's a process whereby you see a series of unplanned occurrences or accidents, you shut operations down, and troubleshoot to find out the source of the problems.

During the stand-down there was a packet issued to all employees. In it there was a whistleblower policy: anybody who knows of a situation of waste, fraud, or abuse or unsafe practice can at their discretion, blow the whistle on management by going to some outside agency. There was a regulation through the Department of Labor that supports this action. This is the first time we'd seen such a thing. In the packet there was a document we had to sign that said we were responsible for our safety and others. I objected to that because management was not asked to sign this, nor had they supplied all the resources for me to be able to insure that I was secure and safe, nor could I be responsible for someone else's misdeeds. I signed it but with objections. They didn't appreciate that but didn't complain. I asked for a response in a meeting that never happened.

I outlined a series of problems that I thought needed to be corrected. This was July, and towards August I received my performance appraisal. For the first time in my career I received a negative comment in my performance appraisal. It wasn't so much a negative comment as an observation. Then I saw another article in the paper, where Hecker [Lab director from 1986 to 1997] said we rely on the audits and assessments area to give us the information. From my experience and prior career, I saw this as a maneuver to position themselves to point the finger at a function. Pass the buck. Since I was in the audits and assessment area and I was the one doing all the audits for the quality assurance, the finger was being pointed at me directly.

I was beginning to see the picture, and after I saw that article I realized that management was not going to be attentive to addressing the issues. They would only point the finger and absolve themselves of the responsibility. The fact was that I had first-hand information that the 31 stacks that Jackson had indicated were in compliance were not. In fact, there were barely two of the 31 that were. Their usual excuse is that we need more money, but the problem never gets solved. I decided at that point to blow the whistle. I started to collect information and put it together in some historical perspective. I made attempts to talk to management about it and they didn't want to hear.

I asked what has been the behavior of the management in addressing these issues? Has anything been resolved? Are they genuinely trying or are they skirting the issues? I collected all the information and then started to write and put together a statement. It was at this time that I learned that Concerned Citizens for Nuclear Safety had a lawsuit going. I thought maybe I could submit my statement to them and they could pass it along to the judge. I debated it long and hard. When I decided to go ahead, I did it on my own. I finalized my statement and made sure I could substantiate every claim. By October of 1996 I submitted it to CCNS and sent a copy to Bingaman and Richardson. I was requesting their help but never heard from them.

CCNS was concluding an environmental lawsuit that began way back in 1991. It was an environmental issue. Another individual, David Nachamson, had blown the whistle. He had brought some very significant issues forward and management ignored them. He was retaliated against and removed from his position. He filed a suit and CCNS supported him.

Based on the information that I submitted through CCNS to the judge, it was acknowledged that the Lab had lied to the plaintiff several times. CCNS then requested information from the Lab based on the information that I had presented, and based on that they were able to determine that the Lab had lied and consequently the judge ruled against it.

I didn't expect that to happen. But the Lab never called me in, never said or did anything. This was the end of '96; now we get into '97. I'm assuming everything's going OK, despite the fact that it was revealed in the paper that I had submitted the affidavit. I'm waiting for the other shoe to drop but nothing happens. It wasn't until I got the [annual] performance appraisal in August that I saw any reprisals. The comment related to the fact that managers were upset with me because I was airing dirty laundry in public. I did what the whistleblowing policy allowed. I was only following what the director said we could do, so this should not be in my record. First of all, it's unrelated to my work, and secondly, I'm protected by the law. I wrote a memo to my supervisor asking him to explain the comment and objecting in general. When he delivered my paycheck, he said the comments had nothing to do with my performance. My salary rating was 2.75 and I had just gotten my Masters. I had high performance evaluations, so my salary just wasn't keeping up with my performance level. I decided to file an official complaint with the Department of Labor.

On November 21 [1997] I faxed my complaint to Kansas City. I spoke to the DOE first to see what the process was, what I could expect, and they told me they were understaffed and it would take them a year just to get to me. By February of '98 I got a ruling; the DOL corroborated everything that I said and agreed that I had been retaliated against. They asked the Lab to reinstate my retroactive salary to the average, which was 4.0, and to remove the negative comment from my record. They also asked for monies for emotional distress and also wanted some written assurance that I would not be retaliated against in the future. The Lab did its usual thing and appealed the ruling. My hearing came up a year later, five full days. By June of 1999 I got a ruling from the judge and he again corroborated everything. He wrote a 72-page order against the Lab. The Lab appealed again and we just finished another appeal brief in March and it now goes in front of an appeals board. We are awaiting the results of that three-judge panel. [Joe was eventually awarded a settlement after filing two lawsuits over poor evaluations in 2008.]

I had a call from the House Commerce Committee right after the Cerro Grande fire. They called me at 6:00 a.m. to say they wanted me in Washington to testify about the retaliation that I was experiencing. I said if you get the plane tickets and the hotel, etc., I'll be there. I talked about the fact that DOE really doesn't have a zero tolerance for retaliation. Instead of helping the employee, the DOE is siding with the University of California and providing money and support to fight people like myself. The zero tolerance policy is a sham.

I understand that one of the purposes of this interview is to look at how Los Alamos has either ensured the health and safety of its workers or not. In retrospect I have to say that they have given it a lot of lip service. That is not to say that certain individuals haven't earnestly tried to address the issues, but the bureaucracy is unwieldy and doesn't facilitate the concerns. Then you have the political and social environment that comes into play. People in the hierarchy basically don't care. They don't want to hear anything negative about the Lab. Their main concern is to avoid any bad publicity because in reality it is all self-serving. They don't want to lose the UC contract because then their benefit package goes. Another concern I have is that there seems to be a revolving door. A lot of Lab people who are in the environmental safety area used to work for the State and vice versa. Some who retire from the Lab go on to the State as a consultant. In my testimony in Congress I was asked what was creating this problem, and I told them about the revolving door. Look at DOE, we have scientists and senior executives from LANL going to work at high levels in the DOE. Their job is to protect the Lab from critical issues. DOE executives who retire go to the Labs. You have this exchange and theoretically maybe it sounds good. The motives for doing it aren't always so sterling. The whole issue is the intent. We have the same thing with the University of California—board members who have gone to DOE.

Richardson's announcement that the government is now acknowledging nuclear workers' health risks is disingenuous. People continue to forget that he was the Congressman of this 3rd Congressional District for 14 or 18 years and there was always denial about the health risks. These risks were not unknown to him. I personally took these issues to him, as did others, even before the Tiger Team came along. Since the Tiger Team people have been in front of him repeatedly on these issues. For him to come out and say these things was really disingenuous. What would really hurt him would be if people could surface the letters they have sent him and the responses. I would think that would be potentially damaging. That could be all part of a good book.

He put through some legislation for worker compensation and now a group of activists are working to strengthen that legislation and see if they can't get it passed. They felt that his initial proposal was weak and flawed and needed to be beefed up.

It's a balancing act, having to work within the system and still be an advocate for important issues. Any public issue that you address is going to be pointing at the Lab or some individual at the Lab. It's not intentional, it's just because of the structure of the society, the social structure, it's all entwined.

The fundamental philosophy at the Lab is that bigger is better. Funds keep flowing in and keep it perpetually in existence— as opposed to saying that this program has served its function, we can scale it back or eliminate it and address another area of science. People obviously don't want this, particularly in the weapons area they want to keep on designing newer and better weapons.

The numbers published by the Lab's strategic plan a few years back show that 80 to 90 percent of the work is related to weapons. It's pretty close to that. If you look at the environmental issues, they are not just general environmental issues, they are all related to weapons work. The waste and the by-products from the weapons work is what the emphasis is on.

What happens with the weapons program and the military scale-up is that the areas of science that really need to be addressed are being overshadowed. You have two sets of scientists—the physicists who do nothing but weapons and you have the ones in other areas. They don't have the power base to draw more attention to themselves. When you look at the impact they could have on the society, we're really losing out.

Politically, the Lab is so entrenched that in order to make an impact you have to address the political structure and environment. You have to expose that and know what's going on. For instance, one of the reasons that they don't want the University of California to lose the management contract is that Bingaman and Domenici really control the place. It's their Lab. If they were to get some other contractor here, it would dilute their power base because they would then have to contend with other political forces.

You really need to look at who the guys are pulling the strings and who are the puppets. This issue with the security is all a political play. Richardson is going to look to see how he can regain some power base from this. He's not about to let the UC contract go because they hurt him; he's going to turn the tables. These guys are either lawyers or career politicians. One of the ways to diffuse an issue is to co-opt it. Don't just hit Los Alamos but hit the whole DOE complex. Diffuse it. It's truly a Los Alamos issue; no other Lab is experiencing this, but they say it's a DOE issue and they support it. They are in bed with the Lab. They scratch each other's back.

Chapter Six

GENE WESTERHOLD

I visited Gene Westerhold in his home in White Rock, New Mexico on June 1st, 2000. It was a sizzling day so we settled on the back porch for our interview. The eaves of the porch were festooned with wind chimes, big ones, little ones, whirligigs and such. My microphone had to strain to record Gene's sonorous voice over this chorus of sound. Once we settled down to talk and his little dog stopped chewing on my electrical cords, Gene had my full attention. He immediately charmed me with his wit and his seamless cadence as a storyteller. He was more than articulate, almost theatrical in his bearing.

It was a long and riveting session and at the end he told about his attempt, after 44 years of service were over, to get his medical files in order to have a better forecast of future health issues. He was treated poorly. His medical records should have been as thick as the telephone book, yet they showed him one page, period, and it was full of lies. Gene prided himself on his loyalty to the Lab; he took chances for them, risked his life, and never asked for special treatment. But now, this was how he was treated and it was deeply hurtful. We honor Gene for his life and work.

GENE WESTERHOLD

Gene Westerhold

My dad was born in 1894 and grew up in the old Westerhold home place down in Missouri. They raised cattle, of course, and hogs. They grew a lot of corn and wheat and other crops. It's quite an interesting place. It was a halfway house for the slaves coming up from the South to the North. It had false walls in it. It had false rooms down in the basement. The slaves would come up and it was one of their stopovers en route north. It has the false walls where you can walk between the rooms in the walls. Then you can go downstairs and there's a tunnel that goes to the barns and another one that goes to the icehouse. Back in those days, people don't realize this, but they had icehouses. These houses were insulated with two-foot thick walls with sawdust in them. In the winter, they would go to the creeks or rivers and take a team and wagon. They would saw out these huge chunks of ice, slide them up on the wagon, and put them in these ice houses. Then they had ice all summer long.

My dad was sixteen years old and he thought there must be a better life out there than looking at the butt end of a mule, so he ran away from home. He got a job with the railroad building bridges. That's how he got into the construction field. After he met my mom he started working on dams and I was born in 1935 in Dubuque, Iowa.

We had a little farm, it was during the War, in a little town 18 miles outside of Paducah, Kentucky. Dad was building the flood control around Paducah and a big powerhouse where the Ohio and the Illinois rivers come together. He had rented a little farm, I think we had about 160 acres. We had a few cows and I know we had a team of mules and a team of horses. I had a saddle horse that I called Daisy. She was an ex-racehorse. I'd ride her the six miles to school. My mom would saddle her in the morning and help me into the saddle and I would ride her to school. They'd saddle her up again after school and I'd ride her home.

We started out with just a few pigs but they kept having piglets, and all of a sudden we had more pigs than we knew what to do with. Of course the War was going on, and there was a big demand for meat. We grew about fifty acres of corn and in that corn, once it got up, we'd go through and plant pumpkins. We had an awful lot of pumpkins and in the fall of the year we'd go out there. I could drive the wagon with the mules, but my dad wouldn't let me drive the wagon with the team of horses. So, we'd take two wagons out and we'd cut and load the wagons with pumpkins. I wasn't real big, about 10 years old, so he did most of it. We'd load the wagons and take them in and stack them at the end of the barn. We had a stack of pumpkins that people couldn't even believe. At night, if Dad wasn't home, my mom and I would go out with these old Army machetes and we'd chop those pumpkins up into little pieces and put them in five gallon buckets with a couple of coffee cans of bran flakes, stir it all up, and feed it to the hogs. That was a couple hours work every night, feeding all these darn hogs.

My dad worked for the Tennessee Valley Authority and was

superintendent of the Center Hill Dam. In 1947 they started the Davis Dam out in Bullhead City, Arizona, on the Colorado River. We left Tennessee and went out there. My dad was super-intendent on that dam, too. Then in 1949, when that one finished up, he was working for an outfit called Utah Construction Company. Well, Utah had a job in Los Alamos, New Mexico building a physics lab, SM-40, and they asked him to transfer up there. He came up and worked for them for a month or two. They incorporated with Lovell and it became Utah Lovell. Well, my dad didn't get on with Mr. Lovell, so he quit them and went to Robert E. McKee. My dad thought the world of the old man McKee, the founder of the Zia Company.

We came to Los Alamos in 1949 and it was a chance for me. Los Alamos High School was brand new and I started there. My dad insisted on staying while I went through high school. I had changed school so much in the lower grades that he didn't want any more changes. In the early fifties they were building all of the permanent Lab. Prior to that it was temporary buildings. This is when they did all the concrete buildings. He worked a lot at S-site. I went all the way through school up there. That was where I met my wife, Shirleene. Her dad was a pipefitter. She and I met our senior year.

The only time we left was in my junior year for three months. McKee had a job going at Fort Killeen, Texas. They had some sort of labor problems and it was a real high security area. He wanted my dad to go down and straighten out the problems, so we left for three months. It was a little farming community. We lived in Belton, Texas, about twenty miles from Fort Killeen. It was quite unique. I'll never forget, I went to this old high school and I had an old homeroom teacher. She had to be up in her seventies. When she heard where I came from, Los Alamos, where they built the bomb, it just fascinated her to no end. So I had to tell all my stories. These kids were all born right there in that little farm town. She thought I was quite unique, having lived all over the country. I teach my kids now about Texas because every morning another kid would get to say a prayer. We actually said prayer in homeroom every morning before we started class. Then we'd sing "The Eyes of Texas are Upon You," and then we'd sing the national anthem. In that order! Texas was something else.

Coming from Los Alamos and going down there, God, I didn't have to do much to keep straight A's. The schools in Los Alamos were really excellent. Of course, I was always a math hound. I enjoyed math and had a lot of background in it.

Shirleene and I went to together during that last year of high school. Right after that, R. E. McKee asked my father to go to Kirtland Air Force Base. They were getting ready to put in a big B-52 hangar and he wanted my dad in on that. So, the day after I graduated we moved to Albuquerque.

That first summer, Shirleene and I visited back and forth a bit. Being a hundred miles apart, it was pretty hard. I went to work for McKee as a carpenter apprentice. I got into Local 1319, the Carpenter's Union and went to work. Everybody in the union knew my dad, knew he was a contractor, knew what he had done, so I automatically went up the ranks in the union. I was supposed to have a four-year apprenticeship, and they would call me in to the examining board and ask me questions. My God, being a kid growing up with it … we had built houses, barns, all my life. Within almost a year they had me up to the journeyman status.

In 1954, Shirleene and I got together again and got married on May 1, 1954 down in Nambe. Her folks were living in a big old adobe house down there. She was working for Zia Company up here in Los Alamos and I had worked for McKee, so we moved to Albuquerque and found an apartment. We lived down there until August. We had just about finished the hangar job. Shirleene's dad was a pipefitter and he wanted me to follow him into the piping trade. He worked at Los Alamos and his best friend, Mose Day, was assistant superintendent up here. They needed apprentices and wanted me to come over. They were paying me journeyman's wages as a carpenter, $3.10 an hour, and they wanted me to come up here as a pipefitter apprentice for $1.65. an hour. I told them, my God, I can't live on that. It's cutting my wages in half.

Anyway, I decided to go ahead and went to work for Zia on Sept. 27, 1954. Of course, living in Los Alamos for years, and my father having a Q clearance, my background was right here most of my life so I got my Q clearance real quick. It went straight through. I hadn't been up here any length of time, and they sent me to an old Tech Area, TA-21. We call it the DP site. This was West: DP West worked plutonium, DP East worked uranium. They were about half a mile apart.

Believe it or not, back in those days they didn't know if they could mix this stuff, so the two sites were split completely. If we went down to DP East we had a set of safety shoes down there in the lockers, and in DP West we had a set up there. They treated it completely separate, not to be mixed.

At DP West I went to work in the plant. They put me with Eddie Hoosier, an old pipefitter who had worked in Building 2 for many years. What they did there was recover spent plutonium. They would dissolve the metals in real strong acids in dry boxes and filter out the plutonium and save it.

It was all kinds of material. They'd have a nuclear shot and they'd pick up all the debris and bring that in and then recover the plutonium from it. So it was a very high acid area and a real high radioactive material area. It was all in tanks and pipes. Everything was transported through pipes. Everything in there was stainless steel piping. Most all of it was welded and highly contaminated. These were some of the most dangerous years that I ever spent working with the Labs.

I was down there that particular time for six or eight months. Then they sent me over to the CMR Building. They had just turned it over to Zia. People probably don't realize this, but back in those days Zia took care of all the maintenance of everything at the Labs. All the new construction was done by the owner,

Robert E. McKee. The new CMR building, as huge as it is, when it was turned over to the Lab it had nothing in it. It was a big old concrete building completely empty.

It was a metallurgical building, a chemistry building built to handle contaminated material. So Zia had to go in and put everything into it. Zia ran all the services, put in all the dry boxes, it was quite a job. So when I left DP the first time and went over there, that's what I did. I worked there for several months and then was sent to S-site, TA-16, which is an explosives area. I worked out there for six months, which was an interesting place. (He laughs) We did some things out there that were unreal.

Back in those days, a tremendous amount of explosives was being poured in the form of different shapes of this and that for building nuclear weapons. They'd take and melt this powder down in big tanks with steam coils on the outside of them. Then they'd pour these molds and machine the parts out of the molds. It was our job to keep the steam going so they could melt the stuff down. Then if they had anything left over they'd pour it down the drain to the holding tanks outside. When it went into the holding tanks it would solidify into chunks of high explosives.

I remember one time as they poured it down it began to solidify in the pipes. Eventually, this six-inch cast iron line got so plugged you couldn't even run water through it. We went in and checked and found that that line was completely solid with high explosives. There was another guy there who I was working with, Buster Freestone, whose stepfather was our foreman, Ernie Bowman. Anyhow, they decided to take these lines out and put in new stainless ones.

They went down and looked at the job. We had guys out there, Jack Converse and Verdie Raper, who were our safetymen. So they took Buster and me down there one afternoon and said, here's what we want to do. We want to cut out all this cast iron line coming from the wash-down pit out to the tanks and we'll put all new stainless steel in there. They'd come up with this new band saw that we could saw the old pipe off into pieces. While you're sawing this out, it's got HE [High Explosives] in it, so you've got to keep water running over the blade at all times. This was about ten feet off the floor.

Buster and I went and got scaffolds and set them up on Monday morning. It was Buildings 300, 302, 304, and 306. We started in 302. He started cutting while I held the water hose. He'd saw a ways, then I'd saw a ways. We finally got the first one sawed through and he said, "How big a chunk do you think we can handle?" I said, "Oh, we can handle three feet without any problem." We start sawing and just about half way through the second cut, I was holding it, or I thought I was, and that darned cast iron broke. It was so heavy I couldn't hold it and it dropped on the top of the scaffold and rolled off. It went down on the concrete floor and we just both closed our eyes knowing that that was the end of it. That piece of cast iron hit and shattered. We looked at each other in amazement, then looked down and there was HE all over. That line was completely full of HE to within one quarter of an inch.

He said, "Let's go over and have a cup of coffee." Between 302 and 304 was a little 10 x 10 building and every morning they'd bring out a pot of coffee, hot chocolate, and cigarettes. This was the only place you were allowed to smoke out there. You couldn't carry any kind of matches. This place had electrical lighters on the wall where you lit your cigarettes. Every morning they'd bring out all sorts of rolls, donuts, the works. We crawled down off of that scaffold, HE all over the floor. We noticed when we went out the door that there didn't seem to be any cars around. We went over to the coffee shack and it was the same thing, not a soul around. We went in, no cigarettes, no coffee. Buster said, "What the hell's going on?"

We decided to go to the shop to talk to Pop [Ernie, the foreman] about that job down there. That was pretty touchy, what we were doing. We went down to the shop, got to the end of the street, and there was a barricade up. We had gone in there that morning and they had barricaded all the area around us, knowing how damned dangerous the job was that we were do-ing! Buster and I never had a clue.

We went in and spoke to Ernie about it. Jack Conrad and oth-ers came over and said they'd tried to think of every way in the world to do the job and be as safe as possible and that this was the best they could come up with. We told them what happened, went back, called janitorial, and cleaned up the mess. We went ahead and cut it all out, in smaller pieces. Every chunk was tak-en down after that by putting an anchor in the ceiling. We'd tie them off with a rope and lower them down like that.

I was out there for about six months and then back down to DP and back into 2 Building with Eddie Hoosier. For protection, believe it or not, we changed out every morning in complete gov-ernment clothing. You could wear nothing personal, no rings or watches: shoes, socks, shorts, coveralls, white skull caps (to pro-tect the hair), all government-issue. Our respiratory protection was a little half mask, usually a Wilson or an Acme brand with little filters in it. I found out, many years later, the filters in those things were made of asbestos!

Anyhow, due to the leaks and the way that stuff was han-dled, the air count in some of these buildings was pretty high. Supposedly we took a nose swipe twice a day, at noon and at night before we left. A lot of times we didn't take them at noon. Just like you're supposed to shower at noon. If we were not actu-ally working with contaminated material, a lot of times we didn't bother, we just showered at night. Never went home without a shower.

Normally we checked ourselves. If we did a hot job, then we had a health tech with us and he would check us at the time. Just to give you an idea of some of the things we ran into, DP was set up in buildings. There were the buildings numbered 1, 2, 3, 4, and 5. Building 3, in later years, worked a lot of uranium. Building 4 had some hot cells where they were working radia-tion. On the other side was the tool room. On the north end of these buildings we had some big cistern type holes in the ground that were bricked in and down at the bottom of these were little acid pumps where our waste was pumped from the cisterns. They were pumped down to a processing plant where they filtered this stuff out on big old mud drums before they turned it loose down into the canyons.

I remember that occasionally we had to go down into these wells to work on these pumps. We'd put on double suits and crawl down in there and work on these pumps. We'd come up so contaminated that they couldn't even get close to us with a Geiger counter. We'd take off the first pair of gloves and first pair of coveralls and then they'd check us. I can remember coming out of there and having the health monitor unscrew the filter and check it in my little half mask, and it would be infinity. He'd dump it in the trash, reach in his back pocket to get a new one, screw it into the respirator, and I'd go right back down there. It was really hot … but nobody seemed to know what it would do to you. It was just part of the everyday routine, you know.

Seemed like Building 2 was the worst. I remember one time a line salted up, by that I mean caustic solution in the pipe solidified. It was 3/4-inch lead pipe, ten feet long that we beat on with hammers, heated with torches, but couldn't free up. So we made up a new section of stainless with flanges on the end, set up scaffolding, and prepared to change it out. Eddie got his end disconnected, then plugged it with a stopper, and taped it off. Just as I was to stopper my end, it broke loose and sprayed me with solution, acid laced with plutonium.

They got me down fast as I started to feel the burning. Got all my clothes and badges off quick and they went in the trash. They rolled out brown paper in front of me and I walked through Building 2 into Building 1 just as naked as a jaybird. Then they threw me in the shower and I started in scrubbing with Versene and a brush. I did that for a long time; then they walked me over to the big Geiger counter that could count up to 100,000 millirems a minute and I couldn't even get near the probe. I read infinity from the soles of my feet on up.

Then they ordered the two health monitors, Henry and Snowball, to get into the shower with me and they scrubbed until the blood came. The readings held at infinity. Finally, they sent me over to Madie Nunn, an old Army nurse, and said she would grease me down with Vaseline, give me bed sheets and government clothes, and send me home. Time was going to do the rest. Here I was, a 26-year-old boy in a lab coat and wooden clogs. That nurse looked at me hard and said, "You know, you're just what I always dreamed of, a nice, clean cut young man that's hotter than Hell!"

Then in 1958 another incident happened. We were working in 218, Eddie Hoosier and I. The operator in 218 was a young man by the name of Cecil Kelly, a crazy nut and a lot of fun. This particular day, late in December, just before New Year's, Eddie and I had finished a little job we were doing. Normally, if we finished up early, we'd go into 218 and sit until 4:00 when we'd head to the showers. We were in there talking to Cecil Kelly. They had just opened the Sundowner in Albuquerque out on Central. It was a little nightclub and motel. They had a big band coming in for New Year's, and somehow Cecil managed to get some of those tickets. They were going like hotcakes. He was so happy about the tickets to hear this big brass band. We noticed it was ten after 4, so we decided to leave. Cecil said I have a batch I have to run real quick before I get out of here. As we were going up the hall to the change room, it seemed like something happened. I don't know if I saw a flash, but something didn't feel right. Anyhow, Eddie and I went up, got a quick shower, and were just about out when the siren went off. Somebody ran in and said they have an ambulance going down to Building 2, Cecil had an accident.

I said, "Oh my God, I wonder what happened." About that time, the evacuation alarm went off and Eddie said, "I don't know but get dressed and let's get the hell out of here." We hurried and left. That night about 6, Mose Day called and told me to report to work at DP: "Don't ask me any questions, I can't tell you anything. Tell Shirleene that you won't be home for a couple of days."

They stopped me at Fire Station 2. I showed them my badge and I was cleared to go in. They said drive down to the old gate, get out of your car, and run as fast as you can to the shop. Our shop was building 31, which was over the hill. It was down at the top end of a little gully. I drove down and then ran like hell to the shop. When I got there, my foreman, Randy Howe, was there. Chris Christensen, Bill Merriman, the Division Leader, a guy named Dr. Baker, were all there, and four or five other pipe-fitters. I asked Chris what was going on. He said, "We had an accident with Kelly. That tank, the one next to the door as you come in, went critical." I asked, "Too much plutonium or what?" "Yeah," he said. "Kelly got a hell of a shot of radiation." I said, "My God, is he going to be all right?" He said, "I don't think so."

There were eight of us, all pipefitters and welders gathered there. They told us what we had to do. We had to make some safe diameter tanks out of 6 inch tubing, put them in a rack where we could transfer the solution out of this huge tank into the safe tanks and cool it down to stop it from possibly going critical again.

In the meantime, they had Kelly up at the hospital and Chris was up there with him. Apparently there had been a build-up of plutonium in this large diameter tank. It was about three feet in diameter and six feet high. It had two big stirrer motors that went down in it, rods with stirrer motors on the end. Apparently Kelly was getting ready to mix this solution and the switch for the stirrer motors was up on the wall. He was kind of short, so he stepped up on his stool and reached up and hit the but-ton. When the stirrer motors started and pulled up the solution into a vortex, the shape of the vortex with that much plutonium in it went critical. It flashed and knocked him off his stool. He thought he'd gotten an electrical shock. As the solution settled down, the criticality stopped. Kelly picked up an old broom han-dle and reached up with it and hit the button again. Same thing happened.

He managed to leave the room and went into 218 quite stunned, almost in a trance. Rod Day and Joe Roybal, two operators, were in there. Rob grabbed him and asked him what was the matter. Kelly told him he was burning up. Rob reached up and pulled the emergency shower, thinking he had gotten drenched with acid. When the cold water hit Cecil, he passed out. Joe Mascareñas was the monitor and he called in what he thought was a spill in 218, but he checked all over and couldn't find any contamination. He was checking for alpha. They called up front and told them what had happened to Kelly. Chris was in Bill Merriman's office and he ran down real quick. He thought that maybe something had gone critical. He had what we call the "cutie pie," an instrument for measuring radiation. As he ran by his office he clicked it on and it pegged [reached the limit]. He knew then that something had gone critical. That's when he hit the evacuation alarm.

That night we worked straight through. The next morning about 2 a.m. we had these racks of safe diameter tanks. We moved them into the hallway and punched some holes through the wall and punched some pipe in there. All the fitters went back to the shop and Bill, Chris, and Dr. Baker gathered us together. Baker was the Associate Director of the Lab at that time. Baker went by and shook all the men's hands for working around the clock to build the tanks and prepare for the next part of the job. He said, "We have to go into 218 and make the tie-ins to the existing lines in order to be able to transfer that solution out. We need a couple of volunteers. You people know so much more about it than we do. Anybody who volunteers, it's strictly on your own. It's a life-threatening situation."

There's Eddie Hoosier, that nut, he elbows me and says, "You know, that's our building. I'll volunteer to go in if you will." I said, "Eddie … ." He said, "Well, it would probably be better for us to go in since we know what we're doing and they don't." I said, "O.K., I'll go in," and we told Baker. The rest of the guys were thanked and Baker told them straight out, "What you guys did, if there was any way in the world I could pay you, I would. You went out and did the unbelievable getting these tanks ready." They all went home.

He then said he wanted to talk to us. After everybody had left, he repeated that this was strictly voluntary. "If something happens in that solution it could go critical again. If it does, it will cost you your life." We understood. "Well, why don't you go home and be with your family for a couple of hours, and come back in and at five o'clock a.m. we'll make the tie-ins before the rest of the town wakes up."

We went in that morning at five. Well, all the material to build these tanks, all the fittings, was in the equipment room at 2 Building where this tank had gone critical. It was right underneath this tank in the equipment room. So Eddie and I went over that night to get all our fittings. Before we went over, Bill Romero, who was our head H. I. [health inspector], gave the two of us a dosimeter to put in our pockets. He said, you all hurry because it's hot. We took a pickup and backed right up to the equipment room, ran down in there and just started throwing boxes of flanges, tees, and nineties, then jumped back in the truck and tore out of there towards the shop. Eddie said that's good, we was in there less than three minutes. He pulled out his dosimeter and looked at it and said, "Wow!" I asked him what he'd picked up? He said 11.4 R. I got 11.6R. We got over to the shop and Bill took our dosimeters and showed them to Dr. Baker. He said that the radiation levels were awfully high and asked Baker what we were going to do about it. "Are we going to keep records of this?" Baker asked. "We all are going to pick up some high levels of radiation. Let's don't even bother to keep track of it." Had a little cardboard box of these used dosimeters and he just threw them in there and that was it.

Chris went with me into 213 to tie in the solution line. Bill Merriman went with Eddie into 218 to tie in the vacuum line. Any lab is kind of spooky looking when nobody's working in it.

All the gloveboxes and the gloves were hanging out, and knowing what we were there for, made it kind of scary. The tension was so high. I was standing on the top of a dry box. I had to take a 90-degree [fitting] out, put in a tee, and then put a new line into the tee. While I was doing this I dropped a $\frac{1}{2}$-inch nut from one of the bolts and it hit the top of the dry box. Chris just let out a scream, that's how tightly wound-up we were. We managed to get the work done. Dr. Baker thanked us and Eddie and I went on home. They started up the vacuum and sucked the solution out of the tank. As soon as it got into the safe tanks, the radiation level dropped fast and everything was all right.

Cecil Kelly died 22 hours later. He had received over 1000R [Rems].

By the time we were actually doing the work we didn't even have a dosimeter on us. See, this is the thing that bothered me when I retired, these two incidents. It comes back to what I was saying earlier, so much of this was done by trial and error; we didn't know. Back in those days it was different than today. Now if something went critical they'd evacuate Los Alamos, they'd talk about it for months, they'd spend a couple of billion dollars, and then probably go in there and do it the same way we did it way back then. Back in those days, if something happened, you took care of it immediately, on the spot. There was no publicity, it never did get out. Security was different.

I retired from the Lab, on May 28th, 1998, and a couple of weeks prior to that I went in for my last physical. They had a form they wanted me to sign. I told them I wasn't going to sign any kind of form, or medical release: "I spent my whole life since I was 18 years old right here at the Lab and I ain't signing nothing. I do have some questions. Years ago I received a lot of surface contamination on several occasions. Three times, to my knowledge, I received a lifetime dosage of radiation. I'd like to talk to one of the doctors about it." They said, OK, they would arrange an appointment. A couple of weeks later they called and told me to come in to discuss my records with a doctor.

I went up and this guy came out and introduced himself as a physicist, not an M.D.: "They called me in to explain your radiation exposures." We sat down in an office and he pulled out this sheet of paper. He said, "I was going over your records, and it looks to me like you've never really had anything." I looked at him and said, "What do you mean?" "Well, back in the fifties you had a nose count, 32 counts a minute." [A swab is taken of each nostril and analyzed to determine what the intake from the air has been into the respiratory system.] I said, "Wait a minute, what are you talking about? Back in the fifties, to my knowledge, they didn't keep records, but in those times when I was at DP West, I had a daily count of 150 to 300 in each nostril. We had spills down there where I had counts that were 4 to 5,000 in each nostril! What are you reading?"

He said, "You must be mistaken, I've got these records here." I said, "You ain't got my records, mister." "You don't show any high dosage at all." "My God, 150 to 250 count daily, everybody turned it in." "No, you must be mistaken." I said, "What about my radiation?" He said, "Well, we don't show any signs of your ever having any." I told him, "Look, I don't know where you're coming from, I don't know what your idea is. I didn't come here with the intentions of causing the Lab any trouble. For my own peace of mind I wanted to know what all this exposure was going to do to me." He kept denying, and I got up and walked out. There was no sense in wasting my breath. He was rude. In another way, he acted like he was trying to cover something up. I had no intention of suing the Lab or giving anyone a hard time, all I wanted was someone to be straight with me and say Gene, over the years this might lead to something. Be honest, that's all.

This probably upset me more than anything. You work 44 years up there in some of this stuff and some of it was bad. We worked with solvents of every kind, like trichloroethylene, my God, we did everything but drink it. All I asked was a simple question. Maybe I was asking it in the wrong way. Maybe they thought I was implying that I wanted to sue. That was not my intention at all. All I wanted to know was what is it going to do to me in the years to come?

Today, everybody asks, did they hide the records? Back in those days, I don't think there was any intention of hiding records. We had a job to do, damn it, you jumped in there and did it and let the chips fall. We had a bad situation, we got in there and cleaned it up and got out. But even if records weren't kept, you know, somewhere down the damned line I know there's some sort of documentation that this incident happened. This wasn't kicked under a rug somewhere. I went to Rad 2 training [radiation safety] and schools later, and they bring up this Kelly incident. It's a known quantity. Everybody who was associated with it knew that Eddie and I were the two that went in and made the tie-ins that morning. Why the Lab wants to ignore the fact that we might have got a good shot of radiation, hell, I don't know. When a man can't be honest and get an honest answer about your health working for somebody, then there's something the matter.

I guess if I've got any pet peeves, it's with the U.S. government for letting asbestos go as far as it did. They knew from way back in the 40's that asbestos was cancer causing. So, they just didn't tell anybody. It wasn't until the late 70's when we first got the word that asbestos was carcinogenic and to quit using it and protect ourselves around it. Prior to that we used to go in with baleen hammers and beat this insulation off of the piping. We'd come out of these little equipment rooms looking like snowmen, just completely white with asbestos. We didn't wear a damned thing for protection. We'd go down to the shop, take the air hose, and blow ourselves off. Put it up in the air and sit down at the table and eat our dinner. Now all of my friends, Jackie Moore died of asbestosis, Mr. Whitson died of the same, Mr. Stuart the same, Stormy Walsh, he was older but had it, too. His son Bill Walsh is still alive and has it. If anybody ever got screwed around on anything, it was the asbestos workers and the pipefitters with this asbestos thing. It's a bigger issue than radiation up here. There were so many of us exposed to it. Everything up here has asbestos in it. All these houses that just burned up here [in the Cerro Grande fire in 2000], all their pipe insulation was asbestos. I'm sure there was airborne asbestos in that smoke. They're going to have to treat it as hazardous waste. That's my guess.

A couple of other things bother me. After that incident with Cecil Kelly, they never did check our radiation but Shirleene had two miscarriages after that. We never did have any more children. We were both young … I look back now on some of the things and I really wonder about some of it.

But like I say, honest to God, I really don't think back then that anybody tried to cover anything up. Nothing was intentional. We had a job to do, we rolled up our sleeves, and did it. Now, people question the past. They might be trying to hide things from us now, but not back then.

We did that job but I'm to the point now where I feel like 60 or 65 is too young to be laying down and dying. Some of this is getting to us. What I've done is done. It's in the past, but if I'm going to go through a bunch of medical procedures and expenses, I think the Lab or somebody should pick up the bills.

We did all that and I have no regrets. I'd do it again if I had to. We did it and it's there and I think someone should look after the guys who did it. I'm not speaking so much for myself. They went and got a couple of hundred thousand for the guys with beryllium poisoning and that's wonderful, but I think the medical should have been worth more. When a person is dying of cancer two hundred thousand dollars doesn't go very far.

CONCLUSION

Try as I may to tie this project up into a neat little package, I can't manage to do it. I recognize certain themes that have emerged: how it was for workers to live in two worlds, Los Alamos and the Española Valley; the divisions between the Hispanics and Anglos; and pride and patriotism that many felt about their jobs at the Lab. I also recognize from my modest sampling of the work force that there seems to be an even split between those who loved the Laboratory and those who loathed it. None of this inquiry has been black and white.

Jobs were critical in the early years to the Hispanic villagers and changed their life patterns from migrant labor to stable, full-time work at home. Work became the focal point of most people's lives. They worked long hours and in the case of Leo Vigil at TA- 49, around the clock. These men and women gave their all, and in some cases too much. Many of these people worked a full day in Los Alamos and returned to their farms at night to plant, irrigate, and harvest as they has done for generations. Ross Martinez recalled that as a young boy his job was to hold a lantern in the dark to help his father irrigate the fields. When it was your turn to get the water, you took it regardless of circumstance. I marveled at this generation that seemed to live and thrive in two worlds.

The workers had real pride in their work. They might have had less formal education but they brought tremendous talent to the Lab nonetheless. Their rural lifestyles demanded that they learn to build, to fix, and create what they needed. They honed their mechanical skills that were invaluable in the long journey toward the development of the bomb. They worked on massive projects like the collider right down to microfilaments that were attached to bomb casings to measure stress. They routinely worked to tolerances measured in thousandths of an inch.

Jonathan Garcia, even though he was working in the most

dangerous of situations, had a certain bravado in relation to his work, as well as a lot of discipline, to be sure. As a heavy equipment operator at Area G, he buried endless amounts of radioactive objects with the utmost care. His supervisors would occasionally push him to cut corners and work faster, but he wasn't buying it. He maintained his standards all along.

When it came to relations between ethnicities people had a variety of opinions. Ruben Montoya was extremely talented at his work as a metallurgist, and it was his ability to do what his superiors couldn't achieve that was his undoing. He became so outraged by their treatment of him that he finally had to leave. He overheard one of the scientists refer to his people as "aborigines" and that was enough. Others like Joe Mascareñas took a more philosophical attitude about what they saw. Young Anglos would be hired and quickly climb the ladder, while senior Hispanics were paid less. But despite this insult, Joe queried, what does the young man have? A rented house, no family nearby to comfort him, and only a good paycheck. I have my family, my ranch, my animals, my church, and my community; I am rich.

One man who reflected on the Lab said, "The devil is dancing on the Hill." I think he meant that people were seduced by higher wages than they could get anywhere else and began buying houses, vehicles, and becoming prisoners of mortgage and credit card debt. Materialism took over. Carlos Vasquez, in his 1995 oral history study called "Impact Los Alamos" examines the effects the Lab has on the lives of the Hispanic workers. He asks, how do people work in one world and live in another? What is the psychic price one pays? In my inquiries on racial issues I found evidence that white and brown have learned how to work together fairly amicably. They don't, however, tend to socialize after work and visit one another's homes. Certain barriers remain in place after all these years.

Patriotism was voiced by a few. Ralph Partridge felt his technical work with bomb tests subjected him to a certain degree of danger and that was his way of making a sacrifice for the well being of the nation. Ben Maestas said he was thrilled to be a young Hispanic who was given the rare opportunity to work in bomb assembly. He felt he was doing his duty and was very proud, as was his family. Later in life he looked back and began to question the whole effort. What were we doing? Leo Vigil, a religious man, also reflected on his forty years hauling hot material and wondered whether the dropping of the bomb was a good thing. The thought of all those innocent Japanese people being incinerated plagued him. We see a pattern of men beginning their working lives with enthusiasm and a strong sense of patriotism but winding up having some misgivings when all was said and done.

In the last analysis Los Alamos was a dangerous place to work for many people. Our list of deceased workers who died prematurely is only the tip of the iceberg. Most residents of Los Alamos firmly believe that the cancer incidences in Los Alamos generally are well within normal range, but they surely aren't "normal" in the Española Valley, where there have been numerous cases of cancer throughout the decades. I heard a woman speak some years back at one of our meetings about her thyroid cancer. She ascribed her illness to her great love as a child of hiking in all the contaminated canyons of the community. She owned a pharmacy and wore a scarf around her neck to hide the scars from the operation; she was surprised to see that many of her customers came in wearing similar scarves for the same purpose.

There was a clear dichotomy between the workers who were lucky and those who weren't. The latter are mostly gone, so we rely on relatives to keep their memories alive and tell their stories. This is a grim reality of Los Alamos that is often overlooked. I've spoken to several men who told me they worked on a crew of five or six and they are the lone survivors. These are men who died before their time of a variety of cancers. And yet half of our informants tell us that the Lab couldn't be beat, that it was a real godsend. We can only conclude that the Lab was a different thing to different people. It did a lot of good, and it did a lot that was bad. And people leave this earth with little recognition of the sacrifices that were made.

Jay Wechsler, a weapons scientist, had this to say: "We have enough weapons. I was in weapons for 50 years. Well, we have enough of them. And we have all this talent up here. We have this tremendous wealth of talent, and many of these scientists would drop what they are doing in weapons in a minute if the political realities would allow them to turn their skills to something much more relevant to our lives."

These are merely little nuggets that don't fit neatly into a pattern. So I leave them as they are, for you, the reader, to sort out. I can only say that sitting down with all these people was a great privilege and this small book is my way of repaying their kindness and generosity.

LASTING IMPRESSIONS

I want to highlight these nine people who we have lost in the years after the completion of the oral history project.

Leo Vigil was a fighter, fearless when it came to confronting authority. Leo worked transporting hot material for 40-odd years and managed to survive all those exposures.

I went to see Leo when I heard that he was dying and I pulled into the driveway to see eight or nine cars there. I thought, oh Lord, I'm too late but it turned out to be a contingent of church people who had come to pray for him. After they dispersed I had a quiet visit with my old friend. I had brought a few pictures that I thought he might like to see. They were of the demolition of D Building in the 50s. It was one of the most contaminated plutonium buildings in Los Alamos. Men were dismantling the roof in one photo and loading section of walls onto a huge flatbed truck. One photo showed a truck all wrapped up in tarps and ready to go to the hot dump. The five-man crew was suited up and wore heavy masks, all except one. The driver sat supervising, with no mask at all, which allowed us to see his face. Leo leaned in close and said, "That's me."

Gene Westerhold has already been highlighted in this book. He was a gracious and generous soul who gave freely to others. My great regret is that Gene was never afforded the opportunity to explore his own medical records and have a clearer understanding of what was in store for him in the remaining years of his life.

Ben Maestas had a bit of a reputation of not being too fond of Anglos. I ignored these warnings and drove up to Ojo Caliente to meet him. His modest trailer was filled with books, mainly about Hispanic culture and history. We immediately hit it off. His interview was filled with black humor: on the one hand extolling his accomplishments handling and testing nuclear bombs; on the other hand mocking the bureaucracy and the prejudice that he had to battle in order to be acknowledged for his work. Some years later Ben called me up and wanted to know how I was proceeding on the book. He said he couldn't afford to wait much longer and he wanted some reckoning for his grandkids. Sometime after that I drove up to the house to visit and was shocked to see a strange couple emerge from the place. Ben had passed and these were the new owners.

Mike Padilla was a special member of this family we created. He spoke to me in his office, his refuge. The room was filled with scale models of the planes he had serviced over the years. There were also many Kokopellis sprinkled around the room, a testament to his Native American identity. Mike was severely burned in an accident involving one of his planes. He had to endure years of intense trauma before he could face returning to work. Exhibiting courage and fortitude, he overcame his fears and returned to the roar of the jet engines.

Ralph Partridge was a man of great intellectual strength with a military bearing. He worked on hundreds of bomb tests and had the reputation of being a perfectionist. He viewed his work in the Islands and at the Nevada Test Site as a patriotic duty. He exposed himself to a degree of physical danger to make a contribution to the country's future security.

Gilbert Fuentes was a World War II veteran who fought in Leyte and knew what it was like to dodge machine-gun fire. He came home with the expectation of some preferential treatment at the Lab. He found quite the opposite. He had to fight to get into the Pro Force, one of four Hispanics out of 500. He later became the director of the EEOC and worked hard to give local Hispanics an opportunity for employment. I showed Gilbert several photos and one particularly upset him. It was a picture of the inside of a Lab bus with a soldier checking the identity of the local workers inside. He recalled being on such a bus that was being checked out by an arrogant little Army brat. He was abusing people and Gilbert was furious. He couldn't believe that his people were being treated in such a disrespectful way. His anger was very real as he viewed that photo and relived the incident. It was almost as if it had occurred yesterday, not 50 years ago.

Emelina Grant was one of the original homesteaders. She was frail and a bit confused by the time I sat down with her. But her recollections of that fateful day when the soldiers came to her door remained vivid. They told her she had three days to get out. She left briefly to get help and when she returned she found her few possessions strewn in the yard, most precious of which were her family photos. When she left she couldn't manage to take the large animals, all she could take were the chickens.

Esther Martinez was a celebrity in her Pueblo of San Juan (Ohkay Owingeh). She produced a dictionary of her native language over a period of several years. Her reputation as a storyteller took her around the country as an ambassador of the Pueblo people. She was in her 90s but still strong enough to travel to Washington to receive a prestigious award. She was coming home on McCurdy Road in Española when a drunk driver took her life. It was a tremendous loss for all who knew and loved her.

Robert Campbell was a soft-spoken, understated man who had one of the most critically important jobs in the entire Laboratory. He was the director of bomb testing in the Islands and at the Nevada Test Site. At the end of the interview he made a comment that warmed my heart. He said that the scientists were very wound up in their work and tended to ignore the army of people who were providing them with all the support. Without all these people doing their work, nothing would have gotten done.

"From the time he was diagnosed with solvent encephalopathy and reactive airwaves disease in the late 80s, right up through whistleblower Chuck Montano's public reading in Española on June 5, 2015, Ben [Ortiz] devoted his adult life to holding Los Alamos and DOE accountable for injustices committed in northern New Mexico." [Ken Silver, Ben Ortiz's obituary from the *Valley Daily Post*, July 23, 2015.] Ben was a gentle warrior with great moral authority. Politicians and fellow workers all responded to his integrity and vision.

Emelina Grant and family

WORKERS AND FAMILY MEMBERS INTERVIEWED:

Henry Abeyta	foundry
Jack Aeby	photography and health physics
Herman Agoyo	San Juan Pueblo leader
Kraig Allender	designer of radiation detectors
Rita and Charles Apel	secretary/chemist
Ernesto Archibeque	janitor
Floyd Archuleta	public relations
Harold Archuleta	senior technician
Ruth Archuleta	nurse's aide
Gene Barrington	machinist
Ruben Beavers	pipefitter
Margaret Bell Chambers	historian
Dr. Irene Boone	health physics
Rumaldo Borrego	shipping
Carl Buckland	photographic dosimetry
Louis Burkhardt	physicist
Robert Campbell	nuclear test director
Bengt Carlson	mathematician
Keith Carter	decontamination worker
Ray Casias	water specialist
Richard Chapman	fire chief
Theresa Connaughton	archivist
Loring Cox	housing director
Jan Croasdale	nurse
Carl Cuntz	nuclear proliferation
Winston Dabney	SED
Neil Davis	weapons expert
Felix De Paula	machinist and witness to Trinity
Robert Dinegar	physicist/preacher
Becky Diven	technician
Kitty, Duddy and Francois	wives of scientists
Dwight Dugan	pipefitter
Joe Duran	maintenance supervisor

Gilbert Ferran	health safety
Gilbert Fuentes	procurement officer, head of EEOC
Jerry Fuentes	chemical analyzer
Henry Garcia	Area G
Jonathan Garcia	hot dump
Severo Gonzales	Boy's Ranch
Emelina Grant	homesteader
Barbara Grothus	artist
Ed Grothus	machinist and anti-nuclear activist
Tony Guillen	plutonium worker
Betty Gunther	UPTE
Paul Guthals	radiation cloud sampling
Joe Gutierrez	engineer
Stan Hall	physicist
Ed Hammel	physicist
Leslie Hammel Turk	daughter of deceased physicist
Carol Harris	nurse
Leon Heller	physicist
Warren Hogrebe	machinist
Lois Hudgins	nurse
Evelyn Jacquez	secretary/activist
Jose and Julia Jaramillo	rat lab and property management
Charles Keller	astrophysicist
Jerry Leyba	RCT
Rose Kidd and	
Libby Marcus	San Juan childcare workers
Betty Lilienthal	photographer/author
Glen Lockhart	accountant
Abedon Lopez	administrator
José Lopez	ironworker
Benny Luhan	musician/fireman
Ben Maestas	weapons assembly and laser
Eloy and Lillian Maestas	nuclear sub welder
Reynal Maestas	construction
Raymond Maestas	technician

Bartolo Manzanares	decontamination specialist
A.J. Martinez	machinist
Dorothy Martinez	technician
Emilio Martinez	Pro Force
Estefanita Martinez	San Juan storyteller and homecare worker
Joe Martinez	janitor
Lydia Martinez	executive secretary
Vences Martinez	laborer
Yolanda Martinez	widow
Joe Mascareñas	environmental waste
Chris Mechels	computer expert
Mike Michnovicz	musician/photographer
Carl Mikkelson	machinist
Charles Mills	Pro Force
David Mondragon	union pipefitter
Richard Money	chemist
Chuck Montaño	accountant
Antonio Montoya	RCT
Paul Montoya	plutonium worker
Pete Montoya	fireman
Ruben Montoya	technician
Deesh Narang	nuclear regulatory expert
Eulalia Newton	mailroom director
Ricky Ortega	painter
Ben Ortiz	welder
Darleen Ortiz	college administrator
Frank and Florence Osvath	machinist/secretary
Ralph Partridge	physicist/electrical engineer
Lou Perotti	the Clowns (baseball team)
Richard Ramsey	hot dump
Bonnie Reider	resident/educator
Molly Rodriguez	executive secretary
Barolin Romero	mechanical technician
Myrtle White Romero	medical technician

Evelyn Rose	widow of police chief
Billie and Cordelia Roybal	plutonium and darkroom workers
Bun Ryan	technician, star athlete
David Salazar	machinist
Johnny Salazar	technician
Manual Salazar	disposal supervisor
Anthony Sanchez	decontamination
Luis Sanchez	machinist
Phil Schofield	pyro-chemical technician
Kurt Sickafus	material science
Warren Slade	surveyor
Alex Smith	mercury still
Casey Stevens	master technician, R and D
Roy Stone	photographer
Virginia Stovall	spouse of physicist
Larry and Helen Suydam	physicist and spouse
Stephanie Sydoriak	linguist/spouse of physicist
Jack Thompson	physicist
Bill Todd	geothermal
Leonard Trimmer	machinist
Arturo Trujillo	janitor
Ella Trujillo	widow of machinist
Manny Trujillo	electrical engineer
Vicente Trujillo	weapons technician
Bill Van Buskirk	beryllium specialist
Alvin van Vessem	SED
Bonifacio Vasquez	Pro Force
Doug Venable	physicist
Leo Vigil	nuclear transport
Maria Lorraine Vigil	secretary
Jay Wechsler	weapons developer
Gene Westerhold	pipefitter
Shirleene Westerhold	homemaker
Lloyd Wheat	safety
Albert Wilson	laborer

IN MEMORIAM

OF LANL WORKERS WHO HAVE PASSED AWAY
FROM WORK RELATED ILLNESSES:

George Allen

John Anderson

Fidel Archuleta

Orlando Archuleta

Peggy Barns

Art Beaumont

Norman Benson

Bob Blankenship

Tom Boyd

John Boyer Gene Brisinio

Ed Brundidge

Tom Burns

Ed Canton

William Ralph Carter, Jr.

Arsenio Chavez

Eldon Christensen

Joe Cordova

Bob Cox

Donald Cruz

Rod Day

Fred Doormeyer

Juan Duran

Sonida Duran

Ed Eaton

Larry Ebaugh

Candelaria Esquibel

Al Fernandez

Bill Fox

"Dickie Bird" Frasier

Buddy Gallegos

Clifford Gladwell

Joe D. Gonzales

Leo Green

Leo Guerin

Alex Gutierrez

Jay Edwin Hammel

John Hancock

Joe Holyfield

Eddie Hoosier

Bill Hynes

Frank Jackson

Johnson, J. P. Jones

Cecil Kelly

Frank Kokeraggerman

Bob Kyle

Bob Lanter

Dick Lawrence

Jack La Motte

Francis Longley

Johnny Lopez

Ruben Lopez

Leo Lovato

Mariano Lucero

Sevudeyo Luhan

Gloria Maestas

Alonzo Maiz

Bill Maraman

"Piggie" Martinez

Alfonso Martinez

Benny Martinez

Billy Martinez

Biterbo Martinez

C. O. Martinez

Escolastico Martinez

Gloria Martinez

Horace Martinez

Jesus Martinez

Leo Martinez

Mauricio Martinez

Ramon Martinez

Rudy Martinez

Secondino Martinez

Seth Martinez

Valentine Martinez

Waldo Martinez

Ray Means

Pete Mondragon

Frankie Montoya

Gene Moore

Jackie Moore

Art Morgan

Chester Morris

Mr. Mundiger

Joe Nagels

John Nichols

Qua Nims

Clifford Nordine

Jerry Olivas

Ben Ortiz

Max Ortiz

Bob Osborne

Joe Pacheco

Bob Parish

David Phillips

Irvin Post

Bill Pritchard

Joe Procenio

Pete Puyburn

Bill Rhodes

Luther Rickerson

Bruce Robbins

Sam Roberts

Genaro Rodriguez

Joe Rodriguez

Buck Roger

Danny "Chicago " Romero

Jack Romero

Joe W. Romero

Robert Romero

Victor Romero

Willie Romero

Fernando Roybal

Joe Roybal

Leo Roybal

Tony "Chap" Roybal

Bob Salazar

Jake Salazar

Manuel Salazar

Robert Sandoval

Sam Sandoval

Raymond Schofield

Tom Seaman

J.T. Simmons

Betty Smith

Ron Sogg

William Sol

Cecil Stevens

Mr. Stuart

George Sweeney

Bob Thompson

Jerry Tenney

Jose Lucas Trujillo

Toby Trujillo

Bartolo Valdez

Bill Van Buskirk

Marvin Van Buskirk

Alex Vigil

Amarante Vigil

Bob Vigil

Joe Vigil

Robert Vigil

Silviano Vigil

Bob Walker

Stormy Walsh

Dr. Whipple.

ACKNOWLEDGMENTS

This book might not have come to fruition without the help of my colleague Kay Matthews, longtime editor of *La Jicarita*, a journal of social and environmental justice. Kay and her co-editor Mark Schiller covered many worker-related issues at Los Alamos National Laboratory, and she was the logical partner to help fill in some gaps in the book with her knowledge of the Lab's history and the labor and environmental concerns that have been raised over the years. She also contributed her editing and technical skills in getting the manuscript ready for publication.

Dr. Gail Malmgreen, my sister, added more editorial insights from an outsider's perspective. Her keen perceptions helped substantially. Dr. Johnnye Lewis supported this oral history project from the get go and when the chips were down and money was running out, she used her considerable influence with the CDC to step up and support us the rest of the way. Without her help we would not have made it. Dr. Ken Silver was part of the life's blood of the LAPOWs. He gave freely of his time and considerable expertise to shepherd workers through the bureaucratic maze of the compensation program. Ken developed some very deep friendships among these men and women who sought his help and felt the intense pain of their deaths. Ron Simmons, my life-long friend, provided clarity and sound judgment as he went over the text with a fine toothcomb. My beloved wife, Lucy, never gave up on the dream of making this book a reality. For her tremendous support and patience through the years, I am deeply grateful.

And finally, to the men and women who opened their doors to me and shared the stories of their working lives with such generosity, I owe them everything. They are my super stars, as one by one, they wove a great tapestry of New Mexico history, one that cannot be forgotten.